A. Cleveland (Arthur Cleveland) Coxe

The Paschal

Poems for Passion-tide and Easter

A. Cleveland (Arthur Cleveland) Coxe

The Paschal
Poems for Passion-tide and Easter

ISBN/EAN: 9783741182945

Manufactured in Europe, USA, Canada, Australia, Japa

Cover: Foto ©Andreas Hilbeck / pixelio.de

Manufactured and distributed by brebook publishing software (www.brebook.com)

A. Cleveland (Arthur Cleveland) Coxe

The Paschal

THE PASCHAL

Poems

FOR PASSION-TIDE AND EASTER

BY

A. CLEVELAND COXE

Ecce Agnus Dei

NEW YORK
JAMES POTT & COMPANY
1889

PREFACE.

THE poems here collected have been written, nearly all of them, at the Season they celebrate, in successive years. Some of them were written more than forty years ago. The "Paschal New-Moon," if I recollect, is the oldest of the series.

All that it may be desirable to say as introductory to this book will be found in the Notes. I beg my kind reader to consult them, on points that may require Scripture citations and other references for the elucidation of the text. If any of the poems are worth reading at all, they will be found worth reading more than once, in connection with the Church Lessons of the Season.

The Paschal-Season, as here understood, extends from the appearance of the Paschal New-Moon to the octave of Pentecost, or Trinity Sunday. How sublimely the Christian poet has said—

> " As through a zodiac moves the ritual year
> Of Holy Church : stupendous mysteries,
> Which whoso travels in her bosom eyes,
> As he approaches them, with solemn cheer."

This book is designed to open some of those " stupendous mysteries," especially to minds just beginning to know and love the Church's system, and to feel the attractions of her holy methods for imparting a knowledge of the Scriptures, and of those "truths that wake to perish never." I pray God that all who accept my guidance in these Scriptural Meditations may be helped by it toward that Heavenly City which the glory of the Lord doth lighten, and "the Lamb is the light thereof."

A. C. C.

LEACOTE, RHINEBECK-ON-HUDSON,
April, 1889.

CONTENTS.

	PAGE
PROEM	1
THE PASCHAL NEW-MOON	6
PROPHECY	9
ABEL	11
MELCHIZEDEK	13
THE GREAT HIGH PRIEST	15
MARAH	17
THE TRANSFIGURATION	19
THE GARDEN	22
SPRING RAINS	25
PASCHAL EMBLEMS	27
SYMBOLS IN ART	30
HIDDEN FLOWERS	33
THE SAVIOUR	36
SCRIPTURE TOKENS	38
THE DAY OF PALMS	40
LEAVEN	49
THE WELL-SPRING	51
A HYMN OF FAITH	53
THE ROSE OF SHARON	59
HOLY-WEEK	61
MESSIAH	63
GETHSEMANE	66
THE BETRAYER	69
THE COUNCIL	74
CAIAPHAS	78
PONTIUS PILATE	80
GABBATHA	93
CALVARY	96
FOLLOWING THE LAMB	98
THE CROSS-BEARER	100
THE WAY OF SORROWS	102

CONTENTS.

	PAGE
GOLGOTHA	104
THE MAN OF SORROWS	107
THE CROSS	110
THE THREE CROSSES	112
THE ATONEMENT	116
THE DESIRE OF NATIONS	120
NICODEMUS	122
THE BURIAL	124
THE SEPULCHRE	126
EASTER	129
EASTER IN THE GARDEN	131
THE EASTER EUCHARIST	134
THE BIRD SONG	135
THE BUTTERFLY	137
EASTER-EGGS	139
THE ROYAL YARN	143
EASTER VIRELAY	147
SONG FOR EASTER	149
EASTER IN PATMOS	151
THE ANGELS ON THE ARK	154
RHODA	156
THE WALK TO EMMAUS	159
THE EARTHQUAKE	163
THE MYSTERY OF LIFE	167
EUDORA	170
THE INNOCENTS	173
THE UNBAPTIZED	175
EUTHANASIA	178
A THOUGHT FROM THE FATHERS	182
AMARANTH	184
THE ASCENSION	186
THE UNSPEAKABLE GIFT	188
THE TWO PENTECOSTS	190
WHITSUNDAY	192
HOMEWARD	194
THE GIVER OF LIFE	196
THE TRINITY	195

TO MARY AND ELIZABETH,

IN PARADISE.

PROEM.

1.

The rainbow oft, on tears of April-tide,
  In the sweet week of Easter, we behold ;
Its bow of beauty, like the Crucified
    Bending from heaven, all nature to enfold
    In Love's embrace. Then from that throne of gold,
'Mid iris-lustres, in the highest sphere,
  Seems to bend down its arch of emerolde ;
And Paradise, it seemeth very near,
As if the dwellers there perchance our sighs might hear.

2.

Sweet sisters, in repose ye wear new names,
  Yet let me dream ye hearken. Once, in time,
Ye were my muses, and ev'n more than fame's
    I courted your applause, in youth's glad prime,
    When oft ye listened to my boyish rhyme

With eyes that shone, as now they shine in
    bliss.
  Ah, borne too early to abodes sublime,
Fain would I know ye take it not amiss
Though angels' songs ye hear—to list a lay like
    this.

3.

Ye cannot hear my later songs, alas!
  Ye dearest ones that deign'd to praise my first:
So grieved the Weimar poet, in the glass
    Of memory gazing on fair forms that nurst
    His young adventure, ere its blossoms burst
In fancy's flowers and fragrance. Such my
    thought
    When for these songs, my last—perchance my
      worst,
I coveted your ear. Yet are they fraught
With His dear Name of Names, who our redemp-
    tion bought.

4.

We grew together, lov'd by one whose pride
  Watched o'er the budding of your loveliness;
Nor knew we, for too soon, alas! ye died,
    All that he wrought our tender years to
    bless,
  Mingling wise counsel with his fond caress.
Wisdom and wit were his, and nature gave
    His manly heart a maiden's tenderness;

And Christian hope adorns his lowly grave,
Where, on the field he fell, Christ's soldier, true
 and brave.

5.

Nor less, while your sweet life was link'd with
 mine,
 I shared her love, who o'er your cradle bent
And trained your earliest thought to thoughts
 divine :
 For oft to me her kindly care was lent
 In words of cheer, with gentle warning blent,
When to the poet's shell I tuned my youth.
 She loved all arts the soul that ornament,
And wing'd her nestlings, like young birds for-
 sooth,
To soar aloft betimes and bask in light and truth.

6.

We parted, where the snow-peaks all aglow
 Shone like an opal, and the setting sun
Flamed o'er the Pyrenees, in pleasant Pau,
 Along the vale where restless Gave doth run :
 And as we gazed, each an enraptured one,
'Twas well we heard no voices, save our own ;
 For seem'd our life beginning—when 'twas
 done ;
And with that sunset, oh ! forever flown
Are joys so long we knew, and hopes no longer
 known.

7.

Yet may I glean a moral from that day
  Of parting, and its light o'er mount and glen,
For in the Sun's own clime, the poets say
  He reigns at sunset, wears no crown till then.
  So goes the adage, too, of meaner men ;
The end crowns labour. Welcome life's soft
    eve !
Who sings the Resurrection cries Amen,
As length'ning shadows mark the hour to leave
This life's deceitful scene, for scenes that ne'er
    deceive.

8.

Ev'n as a bird forgets its wonted note
  When death o'ershades its bower, and comes
    no more
The smile that seemed upon its song to dote,
  So when ye slept, my listless hand gave o'er
  And lost its cunning ; for I grieved heart-sore,
Tuneless my shell and unfulfilled my dream.
  Now, faith reproacheth that I thus forbore ;
Wake, languid shell nor moan, by Babel's stream ;
Wake, from the willows wake, to Faith's transporting theme.

9.

Yes, wake my soul, in swan-like notes to sing
  Of that blest home, where, nevermore to die,

TO MARY AND ELIZABETH.

To them that slept comes Life's eternal spring,
  Where Love enthron'd all human tears shall dry,
Hearts claim their kin and brightens eye to eye.
Sweet sisters, ye are safe. For me, how rife
  Perils of conflict, ev'n as years draw nigh
That bring the grateful furlough after strife,
And shines our even-star, the dawn of deathless life.

THE PASCHAL NEW-MOON.

1.

WELCOME thou little bow of light,
Faint gleaming in the Western height
  O'er Day's decline!
Thou, to the busy world of men,
Art but the month begun again;
  But to this eye of mine
Lighted by Faith's diviner ken,
  A season and a sign.

2.

Welcome, reflected in the rill,
Thine image on the waters, chill
  From melting snows:
But brighter, in the depths serene,
Of my glad soul, thy sacred sheen
  The Church's index shows;
Regent of holy-tides, and Queen
  Of Easter's dawn and close.

3.

Thou hast been waited for: the lore
Of holy sages, long before
  Hath marked thy day:

THE PASCHAL NEW-MOON.

For with thy heavenly march sublime,
The Paschal-eve and Paschal-prime
    One Lord, one law, obey;
The Church hath calendar'd thy time,
    And traced thy starry way.

4.

And key-note of her Easter-song,
Is thy sweet tune, thy path along
    In yon blue deep :
We watch thy crescent, till its rim
Is filled with glory to the brim,
    And still our fast we keep ;
Then, tide-like, swells our Easter-hymn,
    Round the whole earth to sweep.

5.

Thou bringest cheer ; thou endest days
Of fast with feast, of plaint with praise,
    Of rue with balm.
Beauty for ashes thou dost bring ;
The oil of joy for sorrowing ;
    For grief thou bringest calm ;
Thou changest tears to triumphing,
    And Litany to Psalm.

6.

The bow of Joseph, thou ! Thy light
Reminds me of the Hebrew's right
    And Egypt's wrong ;

Reminds me of Mosaic priests,
Their hyssop-branch, their bleeding beasts,
    The prophet's goodly throng ;
Their bitter herbs, unleavened feasts,
  And hallelujah-song :

7.

Reminds me of that night of gloom ;
The Twelve, the One, the upper-room ;
    The Bread and Wine :
Of Olivet remindeth me,
Of Kedron and Gethsemane ;
    Of Thee, Redeemer mine !
Thy cross, Thy cries, Thy victory,
  Stupendous love divine.

8.

O Paschal moon, to wax and wane,
Though short thy date, how wide thy reign
    Afar and near.
Thou art the Church's harvest-moon :
She sows in tears, but reapeth, soon,
    A sheaf for every tear.
Shine on ! We catch thy heavenly tune,
    And shout the harvest-cheer.

PROPHECY.

Her seed shall bruise thy head, and thou shalt bruise his heel.—Genesis, iii. 15.

1.

Sweet spring, from clefts of Eden's Rock,
    Fresh'ning its meads that poured,
Grateful to man and herd and flock,
    And birds that stooped and soared;
Bright rill, whose waters crystal-clear
    Ev'n Silo's fount excelled,
And sent, meand'ring far and near,
    Broad brooks thenceforth that well'd:

2.

Oh! fount of life to slake our thirst,
    Four mighty streams that fed;
Fair Paradise that water'd first,
    Then parted, from each head,
To East and West and South and North,
    Bestowing health and youth,
I joy to view, as from their birth,
    Those streams of Light and Truth!

3.

Streams that are one as on they flow,
    From age to age the same,
Yet broader and more glorious grow,
    Rivers of Life their name;
Refreshing earth, reflecting skies
    That smile above and shine,
Till, in the better Paradise,
    They lose their flood divine.

4.

Sweet parable of promised grace,
    The serpent's head to crush;
I love th' unnumber'd rills to trace
    That from that Promise gush;
To see how confluent words of love
    Enlarge their onward tide;
And how, as to that sea above,
    The waters grow and glide;

5.

How prophecy becomes, at last,
    The Gospel in its strength,
Flooding the world, and forth and fast
    To heavenward speeds, at length;
How in that ocean, boundless all,
    Where faith is turned to sight,
The streams of truth and promise fall
    And lose themselves in light.

ABEL.

By it, he being dead, yet speaketh.—HEB. xi. 4.

1.

'TIS at fair Eden's gate, where bright
    Shine the rapt cherubim,
And waves that flaming blade of light,
    Barring the way to Him
Whose fiery Law hath set the sword,
Whose Love the reconciling Word.

2.

Who shall that gate of glory ope
    And Paradise unbar?
Behold the Promised Seed, our Hope;
    Of Life the Morning-Star:
Whose symbol is a lamb that died,
With spotless fleece our shame to hide.

3.

Lo! first of woman born, appear
    Brothers in manly youth,
And to that golden gate draw near,
    Where Mercy shines, and Truth.
Time's earliest Paschal-tide to keep,
One brings the choicest of his sheep.

4.

Anon, their votive altars rise :
　　Faith's altar Abel rears,
And binds the lamb of sacrifice
　　With contrite prayer and tears ;
While for atoning love he pleads,
And views the mystic lamb that bleeds.

5.

· Forth flames the fire of love divine,
　　But, of those altars twain,
On one alone its glories shine :
　　Cold is the pile of Cain,
Where, piled with gourds and berries crude,
God may partake a sinner's food.

6.

Cold is the heart of unbelief
　　That spurns the bleeding Lamb.
But hot is envious hate, and brief
　　Its slighted conscience-qualm.
Abel, faith's earliest martyr, dies,
Yet lives and speaks his sacrifice.

7.

Oh ! dread rehearsal, long before
　　Of Calv'ry's darker day,
When the Good Shepherd came and bore
　　In death our sins away :
When envious hate, with deeper stain,
Renewed the sacrifice of Cain.

MELCHIZEDEK.

HE was the Priest of the Most High God.—GENESIS, xiv. 18.

1.

OUT of the mist of ages comes, unknown,
　His crown'd and mitred mien,
Who evermore, a Priest upon His throne,
　Shall live and reign serene :
The King of righteousness His sceptre shews,
While palms and olives near the Prince of Peace
　disclose.

2.

And Father Abraham bends and bows before
　One greater far than He ;
Forth come the Bread and Wine, prefiguring
　more
　Than feeble sense may see :
The offer'd tithes His sacrifice proclaim,
And His High-priesthood own of everlasting
　Name.

3.

Thus Abraham saw Christ's day. The man of
　woes
　Is Salem's mystic king ;

The King of Righteousness whose names disclos
 Of Peace the Prince and spring:
The wine-press, for our thirst, who comes tread,
And for our hungering souls to break the Livin Bread.

THE GREAT HIGH PRIEST.

A PRIEST upon his throne.—ZECH. vi. 13.

1.

'MID Alpine peaks, a hoary height and lone
   Oft makes the morn its crown,
Bright o'er the mists. So shines the heavenly throne
   Where Abram's faith bows down,
And comes — tremendous Name — God's own High Priest,
   With faith's mysterious feast.
Unsired, Unborn, the Wonderful and dread,
   He brings forth Wine and Bread,
Which, on that spot, he means to give afresh,
Disclosed at last and known, th' Eternal Word made flesh.

2.

In Salem's upper-room, that awful night,
   See One with twelve recline.
With bitter herbs they keep the Paschal rite:
   Then takes He Bread and Wine.
Think, O my soul, 'tis He, the very same,
   Melchizedek His Name,

The Man that is God's fellow, from of yore,
    All human priests before,
Whom Abram met and own'd mankind's Desire
Who blest that faithful man of faithful men th
    Sire.

3.

We, then, his sons, as Father Abraham bent,
    To Salem's Prince bow down ;
To Salem's Great High Priest our souls present
    And own His Cross and Crown.
His piercèd hands we kiss, and piercèd feet ;
    For offertory meet,
Our alms, our hearts, ourselves bestow,
    And all our pride down throw,
Athirst for God, and crying to be fed
Lord give us ever more Thyself, the Living Breac

4.

For Oh ! once more, where thrones confess th
    shock,
    Our eyes shall see the same,
Ancient of Days, of ages the great Rock,
    Who comes on wheels of flame !
Serene He reigns o'er earth and earthly things,
    The Lord, and King of Kings ;
And sits, a priest upon His throne,
    Th' unchanging priest and lone
The Order of Melchizedek sublime
Before all worlds who bore, and bears beyond a
    time.

MARAH.

The waters of Marah.... were bitter: therefore the name of it was called Marah.... And the Lord shewed him a tree, which when he had cast into the waters, the waters were made sweet.—Exod. xv. 23-25.

1.

The Branch that sweetens Marah's wells,
Of Mary and Messiah tells:
How she, whom all mankind shall bless,
Yet shared our nature's bitterness,
Till He, upon her breast that lay,
Took the sad taint of Eve away.

2.

Hark! o'er the Erythrèan main,
'Tis Miriam's timbrel flings the strain,
Prelusive, to the faithful ear,
Of Mary's song and rapture clear;
For Miriam's name and Miriam's woe
Alike the taintless Maid foreshow.

3.

The Sun with healing in His wings,
The Branch from David's root that springs,

Of Gilead's Tree the spicy fare,
The balm and the Physician there,
To Marah and to Miriam give
The touch that bids the leper live.

4.

Mysterious tokens, from afar
That antedate Messiah's Star,
The rapt *Magnificat* foretell,
And shew the Branch to Israel,
Who reigns and speaketh from the Tree,
I am the Lord that healeth thee.

THE TRANSFIGURATION.

Moses and Elias appeared in glory, and spake of His decease which He should accomplish at Jerusalem.—ST. LUKE, ix. 31.

1.

TRANSFIGURED on the height,
　Ere yet two thieves between,
Betwixt two saints in light,
　Behold the Nazarene.
Behold the Lowly One,
　In vesture like the snow,
And glistening like the sun,
　In glory's noontide glow.

2.

From Pisgah's grave afar,
　'Tis Moses hovering here,
And from his fiery car
　Elijah comes anear:
By saints of ancient names,
　From seats of heav'nly rest,
For Peter, John, and James,
　Messiah reigns confest.

3.

Hear Him, th' Incarnate Word,
    Words from high heaven declare:
Son of the Living Lord,
    His Well-Beloved Heir.
Yet talk with Him the twain
    Of death, reproach and loss,
Of thorns and nails the pain,
    Of wormwood and the Cross.

4.

Where naught the faithless eye
    But shame and death can see,
These holy ones descry
    O'er death his victory:
For, in that dazzling blaze,
    The true Shekinah sheen,
Outshining noontide's rays,
    The Cross transformed is seen.

5.

They talk with Him of death,
    Like those who sing the psalm
With harps, and trumpets' breath,
    Of Moses and the Lamb:
Breaks forth St. Peter's tongue,
    He seems to heaven so near,
As if response were sung,
    'Tis blessed to be here.

THE TRANSFIGURATION.

6.

Soon shall this scene recall
    Those blest apostles three,
When bends the God of all,
    In dark Gethsemane:
When, of the Lord of Life,
    The bloody sweat they scan,
And horrours gathering rife
    Around the Son of Man.

7.

Dejected, yet sustained,
    In that mysterious hour,
Scattered, but yet regained,
    When rises Christ with power,
How joys the little flock
    In Tabor's light to see,
Of ages the great Rock,
    The Lamb of Calvary.

THE GARDEN.

They heard the voice of God, walking in the garden in the cool of the day.—Gen. iii. 8.

1.

The flowers are zealous Christians in our clime,
   And oft with their sweet selves they seem to vie,
   Upspringing, as with holy rivalry,
Which shall look cheerfulest at Easter-time.

2.

Therefore, to me, all gardens in the spring,
   Seem Joseph's garden, with religion rife;
   Full of the Resurrection and the Life;
Of teachings full and holy worshipping.

3.

Blest be the darling crocus in its birth,
   That from its icy sepulchre doth burst
   Full of divine ambition to be first
Of all God's flowers, in holy Easter-mirth.

4.

And blest the hyacinth, of varied dyes,
   That forth, all fragrance from a rotten root,
   Like grace from nature's misery, doth shoot,
In the bright season when the Lord did rise.

5.

Yea, blessed be all flowers that come in time
  To deck the Paschal altar; violet,
  Snowdrop, and arbutus, and mosses wet
From rills that cheer the forest with their chime.

6.

There, 'mid the new-sprung grass, I love to walk,
  Or where the upland wood in tender green
  Of its first verdure, like a mist is seen,
Fringing each tiny shrub and wintry stalk;

7.

Where every sunbeam lights a miracle,
  The clothing of each cold unsightly thing,
  The spreading of the hills with carpeting,
The garnishing of moor and rock and fell;

8.

Where near at hand, or down the vista opes
  The view of earliest blossoms, red and white,
  'Mid tints of leafy emerald, dark and light,
And the sun's gilding on the hilly slopes;

9.

Where o'er the landscape everything I see
  Impatient of its deadness, and with power
  Asserting life in its appointed hour,
True to God's call, with wondrous energy:

10.

So, walking in the garden, heard God's voice
  Our fallen parents, but they heard with fear;
  While we, redeemed, exult His call to hear,
And with all nature in His smile rejoice.

11.

For who, that lives by faith in his true heart,
  Knows not the meaning of returning Spring,
  Lifts not toward heaven the soul's aspiring
    wing,
Longs not thus upward dovelike to depart?

12.

Oh! shame, when flowers are Christians and
    athirst
  With all their beauty to adorn the Feast,
  That Christian men should oft be last and
    least,
Though bidden to the marriage-supper first.

SPRING RAINS.

> THERE went up a mist . . . and watered the whole face of the ground. And the Lord God formed man.—GEN. ii. 6, 7.

1.

THE showers of April on the violet's bed,
And on the earliest snowdrop's drooping head,
   And on the new-sprung blade
Of promised harvest, shed—
   How fragrant have they made
Each breeze of the sweet morn that round our
   home hath played!

2.

So every joy of home and love and life,
The tender love of mother, sister, wife,
   The bliss that children bring
To cheer this mortal strife
   And Time's o'ershadowing wing;
These give their fragrance forth in Christ alone,
   our Spring.

3.

'Tis His baptismal shower of love and grace,
Brings forth from dearest friendship's fond embrace,
   And from sweet kindred's ties,

And answering face to face
    With commerce of kind eyes,
The perfume that is best, and all that deepest
    lies.

4.

None know what loves, none know what friend-
    ships mean,
Save they whose life in Christ is hid serene,
    Who live and love in Him!
Only such love, I ween,
    Grows bright as eyes grow dim,
And lives beyond the grave among the Seraphim.

PASCHAL EMBLEMS.

BEGINNING at Moses and all the Prophets, He expounded unto them in all the Scriptures the things concerning Himself.—ST. LUKE, xxiv. 27.

1.

O WHY to those whose art might rainbows throw
   On clouds and shadows of the Law—so rare
   Is given the heart to sketch in colours fair,
Those golden parables the Scriptures show?

2.

Deem not St. Luke the first our Lord to paint;
   For in the Prophets, as in diadems
   That flash and sparkle with imperial gems,
I see His beauty crowned, nor dim nor faint.

3.

And were the pencil mine it should express
   How, year by year, the Holy Week meseems
   A vision multiform, wherein, like dreams,
Angels appear, 'mid bowers of loveliness.

4.

And dullest wits should warm and generous grow
   The tap'stry work of Scripture to perceive;
   Not thread by thread, but as they interweave
Messiah's image, first and last, to show.

5.

Not of His glorious countenance one trace
   Would I of painters borrow. That, for me,
   Shines out in His Evangel, even as He
To those who love Him would reveal His face.

6.

But the red rood in colours would I shrine
   And glorify; as, 'mid the stars, alone,
   That cross shall glitter when the trump is blown;
Ev'n as it glitter'd once to Constantine.

7.

And as a portrait is with brilliants set,
   I would enrich that sign, beneath, above,
   And all around, with emblems of God's love,
Entwined with arabesque and quaint vignette.

8.

Eve's fig-leaves should be figured, sere and strown,
   Poor human arts to hide our sin and shame;
   And coats of skins, whose fleecy snows proclaim
The Lamb can clothe the sinner; He alone.

9.

And Cain's oblation, that high heaven offends,
    Melons and gourds Faith's sacrifice should
        mock,
    While, on the firstling of blest Abel's flock,
The fire of God, in flaming love, descends.

10.

On Jacob's dying eye each form that rose
    And kindled rapture would I trace around ;
    There should the Shepherd and the Stone be
        found,
And Joseph bleeding 'mid his archer foes.

11.

While in far vision, half assuming shape,
    Should Judah's blessing ante-date the day
    That from His vine unbinds and leads away
The ass's foal, and presses its red grape.

12.

And there that Rock should rise, engrav'd of yore
    With Paschal emblems, by the Uzzian's hand,
    That he who runs might read and understand—
Our dear Redeemer lives, for evermore.

SYMBOLS IN ART.

A LIGHT that shineth in a dark place, until the Day dawn and the Day-star arise.—2 PETER, i. 19.

1.

IN an old castle, 'neath the Pyrenees—
    I see ev'n now each height
    Glitt'ring with opal light,
And the rich meads below, the river and the trees;

2.

In that old castle, thro' long corridors,
    The guide me led, one day,
    As 'twere thro' history's way,
Where the dead past revived sad loves and bitter wars.

3.

Behind the arras of a lordly hall
    He brought me, and I stood
    A moment in deep mood,
Where once th' assassin lurked, close crouching by the wall.

4.

Behind the tap'stry, in a dubious light,
    Its rougher side I read,
    Just making out a head,
A hand, and what? 'twas hard to read aright.

5.

And yet, methought, a figure on a hill
    Seemed glittering like a shrine,
    As if some grand design
Were hidden in the woof, but half emerging still.

6.

Blindly I strove its story to descry,
    Its hero or its scheme ;
    But, as in mystic dream,
I felt Messiah's form was on that mountain high.

7.

I felt, but could not see ; for me defied
    Crewel and scarlet thread
    'Mid golden gleams or red,
Those traces faint and rude of Art's untoward
    side.

8.

But when I came that tap'stried hall within,
    Full flash'd, with wondrous sheen,
    The whole transporting scene :
How on my vision blest it shone like Moses' skin !

9.

Brighter than Moses' face, in morning light
    Messiah's form I viewed;
    And what before was crude
Came out in full design, as day deposes night.

10.

No more I spell'd and groped some clue to find
    'Mid weavings deftly wrought;
    Clear was the artist's thought.
Who could not see it all, his eyes indeed were blind.

11.

And as I went, this moral deep I drew:
    Ev'n so, of Holy Writ
    So dark to human wit,
And those twin Testaments, the Old and New,

12.

The Myst'ry is made plain; who runs may read.
    Even on the side severe
    Messiah's signs appear,
Though faintly, in the Law, we trace the Promised Seed.

13.

Yet as in these old patterns of the loom,
    Of yore the prophets wove
    Their tapestry of Love;
Who scans the Gospel-side sees what they meant and Whom.

HIDDEN FLOWERS.

The testimony of Jesus is the spirit of prophecy.

1.

When o'er the Spirit's words I pore intent,
   My soul is like a maid
   That goes a-Maying in the woodland shade,
  Her peering eye down bent,
To spy here, there and everywhere, the flower
That most she covets for her own bright bower.

2.

So everywhere I seek, and always find,
   The fragrant thing I prize,
   The flower of flowers, whose beauty in mine eyes
  Surpasseth every kind
Of plant or gem, or creature blest with grace,
As childhood with its smiles, or woman's face.

3.

I find, as violets are found in Spring,
   Stones and dead leaves amid,
   But all too bright and fragrant to be hid,
  Ev'n so that blessed thing
Where all seems lifeless if our faith be dim,
The name of JESUS, or some trace of Him.

4.

I find my Saviour in the Rock ; the fount
    That gushes from its cleft ;
    In the cross'd hands of Jacob, right and left,
In Moses' Burning Bush and fiery Mount,
In Bread, in Wine, in wood, in nails, in thorns,
In every figure that the Psalms adorns.

5.

And when there pass, athwart the scenery
    dread
    Of the rapt prophet's dream,
    Mysterious shadows, flecking the sunbeam
With something dark and undistinguishèd,
As in the wood that made the iron swim,
So, in the cloud, I still see only Him.

6.

In Miriam's song 'tis Mary's voice I hear ;
    And Marah's bitter well
    Sweet'ned by that fresh Branch of Israel,
Is the foul pool of nature made sincere
In Mary's womb; by Him she did conceive,
The Second Adam, born of the new Eve.

7.

Nor, as my foot along the desert shore
    Treads in old Israel's way,
    Beneath that fire by night and cloud by day,
Fails my fond heart to find, as I explore,

The sands beneath me sparkling with His love,
Ev'n as those symbols of His Truth above.

8.

So, when in Elim's grateful shade I bait,
    The good Physician nigh,
    I count the wells of health that spring hard by,
And then the trees that bear the luscious date,
And find the Seventy, in that grove of palm,
Beside the Twelve Apostles of the Lamb.

9.

'Tis sweet to trace the Gospel in the Law ;
    Faint outlines and obscure
    Like the first crayon traits of portraiture,
Which the great Masters were enforced to draw,
Ere in the amber light of art divine
Transfigured Christ might on their canvas shine.

10.

So ever, as the Book of Life I scan,
    Still be my soul a maid
    Seeking the flower she loves in sun and shade.
I'd rather shout with Eve—"I've found THE
    MAN,"
Four thousand years too soon, than live or die
Without the Faith that breathed in that fond cry.

THE SAVIOUR.

Thou shalt call His Name JOSHUA, for He shall save.

1.

The serpent's head to bruise whose heel shall bleed?
What shall His Name be called—that Promised Seed?
   The oracles were dark,
Yet oft that name was heard as from the curtained Ark.

2.

" Tell me thy Name," the wrestling Jacob cries:
" Why dost thou ask my Name?" the Word replies.
   And Jacob spake, o'erawed—
" This place is Peniel: I saw the face of God."

3.

" Thy name no more henceforth shall Jacob be,
But prince of God, for thou hast power with Me—"
   So spake that tongue of flame;
And Israel knew 'twas God, even from his own new name.

4.

Saviour and God ! a mystic name that weaves
Both words in one, the Son of Nun receives
  As leader of God's band—
Where Moses could not lead—into the Promised
  Land.

5.

Yet, on that Paschal Eve, at Canaan's door,
Comes the true Captain of God's host. Before
  That Joshua divine
The meaner Joshua kneels, a shadow and a sign.

6.

Comes the true Joshua now, the Virgin's Son,
That Saving Name of the Anointed One
  Unfolds prophetic art ;
And Mary kept such things and pondered in her
  heart.

7.

Back on the Pentateuch like morning's fire
His coming flashes light ; and David's lyre,
  Like Moses' face that shined,
Glows with the Saviour's name in mystic words
  enshrined.

8.

As mountains dull thro' all the silent night
Glitter at dawn and show their crests in light,
  So everywhere that Name
Forth from the prophets starts, as in the Day-
  star's flame.

SCRIPTURE TOKENS.

When Moses is read the veil is upon their hearts.

Some fail Messiah's radiant signs to see
    In each prophetic scroll
  Which the old rabbins of the Law unroll.
They read the page of mystic history,
  The flaming Psalm, or Canticle benign,
  As though 'twere human lore, and not divine.

Forgive poor Israelites when souls baptized
    God's glorious Word explore,
  To grope and feel their way and find no more
Than the blind leaders of the circumcised,
  Where Israelites-indeed with rapture scan
  The Son of God, the promised Son of Man.

So everywhere th' anointed eye descries
    A greater Solomon,
  A nobler David, the Almighty One
Whom Abraham saw with Faith's uplifted eyes.
  For not in feasts alone, but, day by day,
  The Scripture, as with sunshine, cheers our way.

And me, Christ's footprints striving oft to trace,
    As following where He led,
  By old prophetic symbols comforted
And plodding onward as with patient pace—
    Me oft a rapture seizes—when I view
    Some veil withdrawn—faith making all things new.

As where they wash the glitt'ring sands for gold
    In bright Golconda's mines,
  Oft 'mid the sparkling grains a diamond shines,
Which the well-shaken sieve with greed must hold ;
    It cannot pass, it is so great a thing—
    And then 'tis claimed for tribute to the king :

So, when some word in Holy Writ shines out,
    Dazzling my ardent sight,
  As 'twere that Indian gem, the Mount-of-Light,
I claim it for my King. 'Tis Christ's, no doubt;
    For claim it lawfully what mortal can ?
    'Tis far beyond the measure of a man.

THE DAY OF PALMS.

> THY King cometh unto thee : He is just and having salvation: lowly and riding upon an ass, and upon a colt, the foal of an ass.—ZECH. ix. 9.

1.

THE Paschal-moon proclaims the Feast is nigh,
   Whose sign in heaven the faithful still obey ;
And as she sails through airy waves on high,
   Cleaving the clouds that break like ocean's spray,
   My soul, like her, finds out its heavenly way,
And walks with God. I taste Siloam's spring ;
   While the high service of this holy day,
This Feast of Palms, prolongs my worshipping,
And all that scene brings back of Salem's triumphing.

2.

A light on Zion of the Spring's sweet morn
   Is glistening from the Temple's every spire ;
An early crowd through each high gate is borne,
   And thronging pilgrims, with insane desire,
   Hither and thither, for their way inquire,
Urged by some strange alarm, they know not why ;
   The truant boy runs past, with soul on fire;
And Judah's mothers, as the surge goes by,
Strain o'er the long highways a vaguely vacant eye.

3.

"Ho, child! what makes thee from thy tasks
  to-day?"
  "Nay, blame me not, thou reverend Saddu-
  cee,
The world goes out to meet Him, for they say
  The Nazarene draws nigh. Nay, hark! 'tis
  He
Outside the Sheep-gate; do not hinder me!
Thou, too, shouldst see Him. With a word He
  can
  Cast out the devils, still the raging sea,
And lately He upcalled a buried man
That had been four days dead!   Hark!" cried
  the boy, and ran.

4.

All this—while bitter Rabbins heard to spurn,
  And mocked with sneers the idly prating
  wight—
A ruler heard and felt within him burn
  The soul that communed once with Christ by
  night.
'Twas Nicodemus; taught to frame aright
The urchin's babble, its intent he knew.
  Anon, upon the Temple's massive height,
Musing and lonely, stood that noble Jew;
There let us stand with him, and all the
  pageant view.

5.

Along the vale, and down green Olivet,
  Judæa's peasants come in straggling throng ;
And one among them on a beast is set,
  In lowly state, yet passing meek along.
  Loudly they chaunt ; and now the mellowed song,
By starts, upon the fitful breeze upswells.
  Unwonted strains the echoing cliffs prolong ;
That rapt hosanna, 'mid Moriah's dells,
Alike strange things recalls and stranger things foretells.

6.

Yestreen the Sabbath closed. To-day the rocks
  Resound with bleatings ; from the emptied fold
The little lambs, in droves and frighted flocks,
  Are led to bleed like Abel's lamb of old.
  Another Lamb comes with them; and behold !
While bitter herbs are for the Paschal bought,
  Tokens abound, and symbols manifold,
That ne'er before unleavened bread was sought,
Or hyssop from the wall, with like fulfilment fraught.

7.

For yonder crowd upsends the very word
  That long agone was heard from Zachary,
Bidding Jerusalem behold her Lord,
  And promising His coming thus should be
  Majestical, in meek humility.

Hosanna! Yes, the very stones outcry;
  And shall the tribes of Jacob sullenly
Refuse hosannas, when, before their eye,
The Son of David comes, and God Himself draws
    nigh?

8.

'Tis thy last Paschal, Salem; fatlings fed
  And turtle-doves anon shall cease to bleed;
For he that thus to sacrifice is led
  Is Abra'm's Lord and Eve's expected Seed.
  He that makes all things new for human need
Comes like the sheep before her shearers dumb
  To bear the thorny crown and barren reed;
Yes, this is He—amid the city's hum,
The patient Paschal Lamb that sayeth—Lo, I
    come.

9.

Though speechless He, thus, to the hurtling
    crowd
  Whispers the Spirit; while from palm and
    bay
They tear green spoils to bear, before Him
    bowed,
  And fragrant things to strew His royal way:
  And clambering youth wave branches freshly
    gay,
Of peaceful olive o'er the Prince of Peace.
  Oh, Paradise! so waves each palmy spray
Thy shining legions bear, in sweet release
Where swells the Paschal Hymn that never more
    shall cease.

10.

All this, the while, full many a faithless eye
   From roof and terrace, faithless still, hath
      seen;
And dull Herodians, trembling at the cry
   Of Pilate's minions, seek what this may mean.
   For now, emerging from the deep ravine,
The pomp hath passed within the ponderous
      gate.
From porch and jealous lattice forth they lean,
Mother and maiden; hoary fathers wait,
Uplifting shrivelled hands, to view this kingly
      state.

11.

"Back, brawling slave. While Cæsar is your
      king
   This shall not be," a mailed centurion said,
And struck to earth a youth, that, clamouring
   He knew not what, his errant comrades led.
   "What next?" a Levite breathed, and shook
      his head;
A Roman knight came prancing by and sneered;
   A flaunting Pharisee deep curses shed
On vulgar skulls, whileas a lawyer leered;
   And close at hand—'twas He—the Nazarene
      appeared.

12.

The foal unloosed from Judah's vine he rides,
   But low derision frights the stumbling beast.

THE DAY OF PALMS.   45

One cries: "A cross is scored on asses' hides:"
 "Yes, mark that token well," responds a
   priest.
 "Nay, father! so 'twas prophesied, at least,
Our King should ride," rejoined one gentle
   tongue.
 'Twas hers that poured the spikenard at the
   feast,
And o'er His feet with streaming tresses hung,
That, much forgiven, loved much, and thus to
   Jesus clung.

13.

Stand thou within this portal, and thine eyes
 Shall see Melchizedek, of ancient day.
Lo! on the ass's foal, in lowliest guise,
 The Man that is God's fellow! Breathless stay,
 And wait with throbbing heart till comes this
   way
The Man of Sorrows. Yes, He draweth near.
 O God! I cannot look without dismay:
His youth is old, and on His cheek the tear
Hath early worn full deep the marks of many a
   year.

14.

Mercy and Majesty! I see God's face
 In this the Son of Man. Divinest thought
Hath in His front its unmistaken trace,
 And His mild eye with Love immense is
   fraught,
 While the shorn lamb is thus to slaughter
   brought,

And bulls of Basan roar with maddened men.
  Joy lights the scribe's dark brow to see Him
      caught
In toils full deftly spread. Why thus, again,
Where late they took up stones, seeks He their
      wolfish den?

15.

" Hosanna to the Son of David!" Yes,
  The shouting people know not what they
      mean;
Yet oft the voice of man doth God's express,
  And as o'er chaos moved the Dove serene,
  So oft in tumult is the Spirit seen.
Hosanna! let the Temple open wide
  Her golden gates, thrice-blessed Nazarene,
To welcome Thee, whom prophets glorified;
For Shiloh is thy name; the sceptre thine beside.

16.

So to His Temple came the Holy One;
  And He who heeded not the people's cheers,
When lisping babes proclaim Him David's Son,
  How tenderly their infant tongues He hears!
  His kindly voice their cherub voices cheers,
And, while blaspheming priests with bitter
      tongue
  Repress the chorus, lo! with loving tears
He owns their homage, long by seers fore-sung,
The perfect praise and pure of babes and suck-
      lings young.

17.

Nor marvel thou if on the backs abhorr'd
  Of thieves, that chaffer'd in the House of Prayer,
Sounded the threshings of that whip of cord,
  Proclaiming that the Temple's Lord was there :
So Judah's Lion riseth from his lair.
Meanwhile the Lamb in all His features shone,
  And that same hour, more wont man's woes to bear,
He healed the sick, assuaged the sufferer's moan,
Leper and blind and lame—all sorrows but His own.

18.

Oh! Lamb of God, that tak'st our sins away,
  So moved the Infinite within Thy breast,
With myst'ries from before Creation's Day,
  Thus to take part in our poor world's unrest ;
  For our relief to be Thyself distressed,
For man's release to be the victim bound !
  Trembling, I worship, my Redeemer blest;
For not, like Thomas, would I probe Thy wound,
Or that abyss explore whose fathom ne'er was found.

19.

Yet bid me meet Thee, from the tomb unsealed,
  And walking to Emmaus ; like a coal

To feel my heart burn in me, when reveal'd
  I see the Law's dread page, the prophet's scroll,
And trace Thy tokens down from Eden's goal:
For thus is purged from rheums and scales as vile
  Man's skeptic eye, and parables unroll
And Psalms unfold Thy Name — each weary mile
Of those that walk with Thee to brighten and beguile.

20.

But lo! the Paschal moonbeam from the East
  On Kedron's rill sheds holy influence bright;
Now cleanse their platters Pharisee and priest,
  Their hearts fermenting still with Cain's despite,
  Their leaven of malice taints the legal rite,
For Joseph's breth'ren hate him. He afar
  Hath gone where Martha's kindly lamp gives light,
And Mary listens with enrapt Lazar,
Till shines o'er Bethany once more the Morning Star.

LEAVEN.

Not the leaven of bread.—St. Matt. xvi. 12.

1.

The moon is full, the moon shines fair ;
The feast is nigh ; of leaven beware !
Unleavened bread be Judah's care.

2.

One crumb of leaven, it taints the whole :
So reads the great Law-giver's scroll,
Confirm'd by Sinai's thunder-roll.

3.

Ye sons of Jacob stand aloof
From Gentile tables ; make sure proof
Of house and home from floor to roof.

4.

Scour cup and platter. Leave no trace ;
Scrape, purge and every spot efface,
Lest leaven be there, so bad and base !

5.

Outside so clean, but all within
Fermenting malice, crime and sin ;
So did th' unleavened days begin.

6.

The leaven of bread is put aside,
But envy, hate, and guile abide,
For Jesus must be crucified !

7.

They would not enter Pilate's hall :
'Twould leaven and defile them all.
Horrours, to think of such a fall !

8.

So taught the scribes, and wonder we
Such blind and senseless rites to see :
We marvel at the Pharisee.

9.

We marvel ; but ourselves, the while,
Doth naught of that old leav'n defile ?
Of malice naught—nor hate, nor guile ?

10.

How dare we, Shepherd of the sheep,
With Thee our Passover to keep,
Unpurified from stains as deep ?

11.

Gracious the Lent and blest the week,
If steadfast, and in duty meek,
Sincerity and truth we seek.

12.

So may we joy to keep the Feast,
From chains of sin and shame released,
With Thee our Prophet, King, and Priest.

THE WELL-SPRING.

THEN Israel sang this song, Spring up, O Well.—NUMB. xxi. 17.

1.

THE great Law-giver smote the Rock:
Forth gushed the waters at the shock,
And Israel drank the wave, as 'twere a shep-
  herd's flock:
  Spring up, O Well!

2.

Nor ceased that Rock to slake their thirst;
It followed them as at the first.
Where'er they went afresh the Rock would burst:
  Spring up, O Well!

3.

No servile toil to dig the sands!
But nobles, with their sceptred hands
Struck the parched soil and spake their mild
  commands:
  Spring up, O Well!

4.

Their princes pierced the arid plain,
And gushed the hidden springs amain;
While Israel's daughters danced and sang the
  strain—
  Spring up, O Well!

5.

That Rock was Christ the Crucified ;
Nor, till the soldier pierced His side,
Knew they what Well of Life it signified :
    Spring up, O Well !

6.

And still along Life's desert way
That Rock yet follows us each day :
We ope that streaming font where'er we pray—
    Spring up, O Well !

7.

The babe that to the font they bring
Invokes again the hidden Spring ;
Those rosy lips, had they but words, would sing :
    Spring up, O Well !

8.

The priest, that in the utmost lands
Before the Christian altar stands,
Says, o'er the crimson'd cup uplifting hands—
    Spring up, O Well !

9.

Oh ! then, to cleanse my soul begin,
Bath of my soul, from shame and sin :
And that I thirst no more, spring up within ;
    Spring up, O Well !

A HYMN OF FAITH.

> How are the dead raised up? and with what body do they come?—1 Cor. xv. 35.
>
> How can these things be?—St. John, iii. 9.
>
> I do not exercise myself in great matters which are too high for me.—Ps. cxxxi. 2.

1.

There are, like that old Pharisee by night,
Who talk, in darkness, with the Light of Light,
Answering, like cuckoos, to each mystery—
      How can it be?

2.

How are the dead raised up?—as 'twere in strife
With Him, the Resurrection and the Life;
As if no mystery to sight and thought
      Were daily brought!

3.

But me, content, the Psalmist's rule restrains,
And from presumptuous words my soul refrains,
Happy may I but live, all undefiled,
      A weanèd child.

4.

For base, at best, that impudence of doubt,
That mocks the Infinite, with searching out;
As if Who wrought of Nature the deep plan
    Were weak as Man.

5.

I would not be more wise than what is writ,
In things that are too high for human wit,
Sublimer far to own th' unbounded Vast
    Around us cast;

6.

Where oft, like men of lore who read the face
Of spangled Night, I seem to feel in space
New worlds, that were not made for mortal eye,
    To Faith draw nigh.

7.

Nor would I follow where, if man hath trod,
Or mounted as on waxen wings to God,
Perchance he ventured towards the throne—
    too near
        For holy fear.

8.

There is a holiest of the holies— where
The seraphs veil their faces, nor would dare
Look curious upward: for the Holy One
    Outshines the sun.

9.

Stone-blind the bard—too bold of mind and eyes
Who there presumed in fancy's flight to rise—
Stone-blind he turn'd : yet sung of Eden's prime
    In dream sublime.

10.

Perchance he err'd, ev'n dreaming, so to blend
With truth his fable, as if truth to mend.
Nor yet, like Dante, would I pass below,
    Where spirits go.

11.

Not me the sibyl's bough or lips should win
Profanely venturing, with the dead in sin,
To follow Virgil and the Florentine
    'Mid depths unseen.

12.

For oh ! what better things, from pride concealed,
Glorious and vast are to the meek revealed :
How oft of Heaven we gain what we forego
    By stooping low.

13.

How oft, in God's stupendous book, unroll
Tokens of things unseen, that lift my soul
Out of earth's dross, beyond this life of sense,
    To realms immense !

14.

How sweet in childlike love to meet Thy test ;
Because Thyself I know, to trust the rest ;
Because Thou mak'st eternity mine own,
    Much to postpone.

15.

Not less where Science bids her tapers burn
It me delights with her to muse and learn,
Discov'ring more and more, in Nature's plan,
    That humbles man.

16.

For He who all things made, makes all things
    new ;
Makes bare His works to prove His word most
    true ;
Upbraids our sloth and saith to sense and sight ;
    Let there be Light.

17.

Hail ! childlike Wisdom, hail Elect of men
Who range through space, as 'twere with angel's
    ken,
Yet own how all that makes progressive lore
    Faith knows before.

18.

A Holy Ark fast closed ! 'Neath Nature's lid,
What worlds of wonder unattained lie hid !
Sure, of all knowledge and all truth—the key
    Is knowing Thee ;

A HYMN OF FAITH.

19.

Is knowing Thee, of Love the Bleeding Lamb;
Is knowing Thee, th' unsearchable I AM;
Is in the soul thy seven-fold gifts to shrine,
    Spirit Divine.

20.

Thine the true Science, Thine the rainbows bright
On Newton's glass where falls one ray of light;
For God is Light, and light in reason's noon
    Is found triune.

21.

Hail, star-eyed Science! Welcome to the choir
Where saints with Seraphim attune the lyre!
Welcome the seer august who comes to prove
    God's earth doth move:

22.

Whose reverent thought, baptiz'd in heavenly dews,
Not less the Moving Hand discerns and views;
Discovers, as he scans the starry zone,
    That naught is known:

23.

Naught but faint whispers from Eternity:
While dark and deep abides the shoreless sea,
Where gleans the sage some shells from Nature's verge,
    Hard by its surge.

24.

Thus let us deal with matter as 'tis meet.
'Tis naught but ashes under Faith's firm feet,
Naught but the nest where grows the Phœnix-
    wing
        Soon forth to spring :

25.

Naught but the cottage frail of moulded clay
Whose shatter'd walls let in some light of day ;
Where yearns the soul in life and light to soar,
        Forevermore.

THE ROSE OF SHARON.

I am the Rose.—CANT. ii. 1.

1.

SOME say Crusaders, in Gethsemane,
   Found blood-red flowers that now grow every-
      where ;
   But me, each thorny rose that scents the air,
Minds of that gory crown on Calvary.

2.

Perhaps 'tis true, from spicy seeds that fell
   At Christ's embalming, 'round the rocky door,
   Even as the Saviour to His rest they bore,
Sprung amaranth and fragrant asphodel.

3.

Howe'er it be, I deem since time began
   The flowers were parables to wounded hearts :
   And still their silent fragrance often starts
Refreshing tears and speaks in signs to man.

4.

They rise in beauty, at our Easter tide,
   From nothingness asserting life anew,
   Rise in all colours bursting into view,
And quickened every one because it died.

5.

I know their meaning. To my gladsome ear
   The voice of God seems most articulate :
   " Ev'n so," it tells me, " let the dead await
My call to rise : in time they too shall hear."

6.

And shall His children then like earth-worms
      grope,
   And bred of earth with earth contented be ?
   Nay, dear Redeemer, Heaven is ours in Thee,
And though we die our flesh shall rest in Hope.

HOLY-WEEK.

> THIS that is glorious is His apparel . . . Mighty to save.
> —ISAIAH, lxiii. *i.*

1.

WHO comes from Edom? Who with garments
   dyed,
   As from the battle comes the conqueror?
Thus, 'mid confusèd noise, the prophet spied
   Far off Immanuel's Day, the crimson gore—
   The battle and the victor-spoils He bore.
Can this the Lion be—this snow-white Lamb,
   That comes from Bozrah; while with wild
     uproar,
The crowds, around Him, lift the wavy palm,
And shout, for David's Son, his sweet hosanna-
   psalm?

2.

Can this be He, the Mighty One to save,
   Who meek and lowly rides the ass's foal?
Such were the tokens Zechariah gave,
   But where the hero of Isaiah's scroll?
   The Victor in the Victim—O my soul,
The Lion in the Lamb have faith to see.
   And hear'st thou not, as 'twere the thunder's
     roll,
The voice prophetic that proclaims—'tis He,
Who comes His war to wage, foretelling Victory?

3.

Thus Faith discerns, in prophecy twofold,
   The Hero-King, the Lamb of lowliest guise:
Nor marvels that his signs are doubly told,
   Whose many crowns are as the starry skies:
   Whose many wounds are countless mysteries.
So Judah's lion is his title, there,
   Where stands on Zion, full of wounds and eyes,
The Lamb once slain : the Lamb our sins to bear,
Nor less the Lion too, our dragon-foe to tear.

4.

For this is He, disclosed in after day,
   On the white horse who rode, with eyes of flame
Him all the armies of the heavens obey,
   Whom Lord of lords and King of kings they claim.
   The seer of Patmos saw them as they came
On snow-white steeds, and robes as white are theirs.
Faithful and true His Everlasting Name :
And diadems upon His head He wears,
Supreme o'er thousand thrones, who God's own glory shares.

MESSIAH.

BECAUSE of the savour of Thy good ointments; Thy Name is as ointment poured forth: therefore do the virgins love Thee.—CANT. i. 3.

1.

No name but Thine, thou bleeding Lamb,
    From earth's foundations known;
No name but Thine, the great I AM,
    Is faith's sure corner-stone.
The martyr's crown, the victor's palm,
And heaven's eternal Paschal Psalm,
    Exalt that name alone.

2.

Thy many ointments, Priest and King,
    Messiah Thee proclaim;
Thee, Samuel's oil of hallowing,
    On David's youth that came.
Jacob's anointed Stone—we sing,
That Rock, the Christ, prefiguring
    Thine own sweet-savoured name.

3.

And many crowns, dear Lord, are Thine;
    Be crowned with Love to-day!
The virgins love Thy names divine;
    The pure in heart are they.

At Simon's feast, where guests recline,
While breaks this loving heart of mine,
   All this the nard shall say.

4.

So Mary mused—and on His head
   Poured forth the sweet perfume;
Silent her lips, but all was said
   When fragrance filled the room.
She gave it for His burial dread,
Whose Name, like precious ointment shed,
   May sweeten ev'n the tomb.

5.

The virgins love Thee. Simon's board
   Shall know with love how deep.
For all who love Thy Name, is poured
   This balm Thy locks to steep :
Ere thorns entwine Thy brow adored,
Ere 'gainst Thy flock awakes the sword,
   Oh, Shepherd of the sheep !

6.

It fills the room ; it fills the earth ;
   Where'er the Promised Seed
Is worshipp'd, in His dew of birth,
   His Gospel tells her deed.
Such meet memorial of her worth,
In Paschal fast and Paschal mirth
   The willing nations read.

7.

For oh ! death reign'd, and Nature's moan
  From babes and children came ;
From kings and cotters, born to groan,
  From poor and proud the same.
Till He the Mighty to atone,
Made Life and Light and glory known,
    By His Anointed Name.

8.

Uprose His Cross ! To mortal eyes
  The Dayspring after Night :
So doth the Morning Star arise
  Where wand'rers hail its light.
Messiah's Name and Sacrifice,
The Christian altar glorifies,
    That shines to Faith so bright.

GETHSEMANE.

> Though He were a Son, yet learned He obedience by the things which He suffered.—Hebrews, v. 8.

1.

'Mid olive groves the lantern gleams,
And water'd glades of Kedron's streams;
With sword and staves and front austere
The lawless band by night draw near,
While Jesus, on the bended knee,
Suffers in lone Gethsemane.

2.

Oh! stand aside; draw not too nigh—
'Tis not for mortal ear nor eye
That conflict or that prayer to scan.
'Tis not for mind, or thought of man:
An angel stoops to bear Him up,
While Jesus drains the Father's cup.

3.

The Man of Sorrows—breathes His moan;
His pangs unknowable, unknown!
A Son, the well-beloved, but still
Content to do His Father's will,
Thrice crying to the Holy One,
"Father, Thy will not mine be done."

4.

Thus in His agonizing swound
His bloody sweat bedews the ground,
And perfect made by human fears
The Man of Sorrows and of Tears,
Of brother men all tears can share,
Our pangs can heal, our guilt may bear.

5.

But clouds have dimmed the Paschal moon ;
Of night draws nigh the sombre noon ;
Heard in the fear His soul that frayed
The Shepherd, where His sheep are laid,
Draws nigh, the drowsy flock to seek,
Of spirit strong, of flesh so weak.

6.

"Could ye not watch with me one hour?
But, oh! of darkness 'tis the power,
Sleep while ye may and take your rest.
But, nay! no more by sloth oppress'd,
Wake, let us go! For lo! at hand
Is he who leads their armed band."

7.

With swords and staves they come—and this
Is he who gives the treach'rous kiss!
"Whom seek ye?" "Jesus!" "I am He,
Let then my harmless flock go free."

The Shepherd smitten—flees the flock,
And trembles he surnamed a Rock.

8.

Lo ! prompt to fight with flesh and blood,
He strikes—to make his promise good,
Yet quails—that bleeding ear restored,
When Jesus bids—" Put up thy sword."
Oh ! slow to learn not steel to bare,
In faith's stern fight of watch and prayer !

9.

Behold the Lamb to slaughter led,
By wolves athirst His blood to shed,
And mute as Paschal victims are,
While Peter follows Him—afar !
Far off he follows Christ, and all
Like him who halt like him must fall.

THE BETRAYER.

They were exceeding sorrowful, and began every one of them to say unto Him, Lord, is it I?—St. Matt. xxiv. 22.

1.

If you fare along the Rhine,
When the moon at full may shine,
    Be sure to halt at Speyer.
And when lights and shadows fall
Hard by the minster wall,
You may see what I recall,
    And admire.

2.

Admire, tho' rude the art,
For it moved my inmost heart,
    And its parable I felt.
It brought to mind that cry
Of apostles—"Is it I?"
And my heart, as I drew nigh,
    Seemed to melt.

3.

Of the river from afar
No murmur came to jar,
    Of the nearer town no hum.

One feels 'tis holy ground,
'Mid the trees and shrubs around,
And a holy awe profound
    Strikes you dumb.

4.

On a knoll, in soft moonlight,
Lo! figures that affright,
    With staves and swords that slay;
Climbing on they seem to go,
Seem moving to and fro,
Like robbers creeping slow,
    To their prey.

5.

Like a serpent's cruel coils
They wind and weave their toils
    Round a hillock clad with palm;
And there, with strange grimace,
Stands one of thievish face,
Who points with finger base
    At the Lamb.

6.

The Lamb of God I scan,
The suffering Son of Man,
    And the angel hov'ring o'er;
As He sinks on bended knee,
Those pangs I seem to see,
Which, all for men like me,
    Jesus bore.

THE BETRAYER.

7.

Seen of angels! So He kneels,
And mine the guilt He feels,
    And it makes me sore afraid;
For oh! that serpent old,
His arts are manifold,
And still is Jesus sold,
    And betrayed.

8.

O Saviour, but for grace,
Is the human heart so base,
    So prompt to go amiss!
As he stands upon the brink,
I look, and seem to shrink
From the traitor, when I think
    Of his kiss!

9.

Is this the man that sate
And with the Saviour ate
    The supper, ev'n to-day!
Whose feet He washed, unclean,
That hasted from the scene,
Swift to shed His blood, I ween,
    And betray?

10.

From a heart that knows no guile,
Who turns supremely vile
    In a moment's fiery flame?

'Tis habit, nurs'd full long,
Makes the last temptation strong,
And breeds the lust of wrong,
    With its shame.

11.

And so from Holy Writ
Comes this warning, fair and fit,
    To the heart of one and all :
Fear and tremble to begin ;
For adding sin to sin,
As gamesters waste to win,
    So men fall.

12.

If the world from pole to pole
One might gain, but lose his soul,
    What the profit with the cost ?
Full many a warning word,
Like this the traitor heard,
For pelf that sold his Lord,
    And was lost.

13.

And oh ! his madden'd mood,
When down the price of blood
    At their feet he dash'd amain—
Who mock'd with scorn and hate,
As forth he rushed to fate;
For repentance came too late,
    And was vain.

14.

But I smite my breast and cry,
Holy Jesus, "Is it I?"
    As I linger long and gaze;
God be merciful to me,
For not the Pharisee,
But the publican I'd be,
    All my days.

15.

'Tis mine—the guilt He feels,
'Neath the angel as He kneels,
    Mine His Father's mystic frown:
Methinks I see it yet,
That brow with dew-drops wet,
And beads of bloody sweat,
    Dropping down!

16.

Tho' rude and crude the art,
It stamped upon my heart
    Such thoughts like coals of fire:
I seem'd indeed to see
A true Gethsemane,
As by chance it came to me,
    There in Speyer.

THE COUNCIL.

Let our strength be our justice.—Wisdom, ii. 11.

1.

Who wrote the Book of Wisdom? From his pen
    Distill'd the ichor of the prophets' lore.
    What Caiaphas would do, he shewed before,
And how they slew the Just, foresaw with keenest ken.

2.

For while the worldly wise proclaimed their dream,
    Should perfect virtue on the earth appear,
    Him all mankind would worship and revere,
What of the human heart did that true wisdom deem?

3.

Ev'n Plato, taught by Scriptures of the Jew,
    Foretold what cruel death the Just should die:
    If seen on earth, Him they would crucify
With shame and scourging: this the sage of Greece foreknew.

4.

Come then, pedestrian muse, while I transcribe
　From Wisdom's page those counsels of the
　　night
　By forecast written, of the high-priests' spite,
With scribe and Pharisee and chiefs of every
　tribe.

5.

Let us oppress the righteous Man—they cry,
　And for the just man lie in wait, because
　He blames us for transgressing our own laws!
He is not of our sort, and sure he ought to die.

6.

And contrary to all our ways is he;
　Rebukes our education and our life;
　Child of the Lord, with other men at strife,
Such is this man self-styled, who chides our
　infamy!

7.

As filth he shuns our ways, as if 'twere his
　Alone to know the Lord! He seemeth made
　Our thoughts to challenge and our deeds
　　upbraid.
We cannot bear a man so just, forsooth, as this.

8.

Grievous to bear the fashion of his ways
　Whose life is not like ours. If he is gold
　Then we are counterfeits! Who can behold
A man so strangely just, nor hate him while they
　gaze!

9.

God is his Father! And he maketh boast
    That such as he are blessed in their end!
    Ha! let us see—if God be this man's friend—
What happens in his end, when help he needeth
    most?

10.

Let then His God deliver this His Son,
    If He will have Him—from the cross and rod!
    Blasphemer! if He be the Son of God,
Then let the Father save from death His Holy
    One.

11.

So they fulfil what law and prophet saith;
    Such things did they imagine—self-deceived,
    And blind through wickedness—such things
        believed;
Let us condemn him then, they said, to shameful
    death.

12.

Of blameless souls they loved not the reward,
    Nor knew God's mysteries; nor wages sought
    Of righteousness—but death, by Satan brought,
While lo! the just shall live immortal with the
    Lord.

13.

So far the Book of Wisdom ; thus they spake,
   As 'twas forewritten. In the midnight dark,
   They wait their victim with their band : and hark !
They come with clamours rude, the welkin that awake.

14.

Last prophet of the Jews—'twas Caiaphas
   Said—" for the Jews, 'twas good, this man should die : "
   Now, let the people hear him prophesy
What Romans next will do ; for so 'twill come to pass.

15.

" They shall come hither and our place make void,
   And take away our Nation." Even so !
   In Rome that arch of Titus still may show
How soon the Romans came and all destroyed.

CAIAPHAS.

The high-priest rent his clothes.—St. Matt. xxvi. 65.

1.

Night in the cruel high-priest's hall
   And night his soul within !
Of Caiaphas—that whited wall,
   Who hath the greater sin,
How blood-stained in the book of time
   The page that doth record
His deed of darkness and of crime,
   Who judged his judge and Lord.

2.

Go read how meekly him before
   The Lamb of Abel stood ;
How he who Aaron's mitre bore
   Could shed Messiah's blood ·
Mere type and shadow of the law
   He scorns the substance true,
And God's High-Priest, whom Abra'm saw,
   This priestly traitor slew.

3.

Aye, read that oracle of flame,
   His victim's answer dread ;
Adjured in great Jehovah's name,
   What God's co-equal said :
Hereafter, thou who judgest Me
   Before My bar shalt stand,

In clouds the Son of Man shalt see
  Enthroned at God's right hand.

4.

The high-priest rent his clothes, but knew
  Not half that rending meant ;
That day, the temple of the Jew,
  That day, its veil was rent.
His shadowy priesthood thus he doff'd
  With that symbolic vest ;
Melchizedek, while yet he scoff'd
  Before him stood confess'd.

5.

Now Caiaphas was he who gave
  This counsel—so it saith—
The people of the Jews to save
  One man should die the death.
Like Balaam's beast he prophesied,
  Nor knew 'twas of the Lord ;
Not of himself he spake, nor lied,
  But voiced the Spirit's word.

6.

Then let the Romans come ; their prey
  Their eagles may consume :
The carcass let them bear away,
  To give the Living room :
For He the one High-Priest must reign
  Whom Caiaphas made known—
The Lamb for all the nations slain,
  And not for Jews alone.

PONTIUS PILATE.

The Priest shall make an Atonement for the soul that sinneth ignorantly and for the stranger that sojourneth among them.—NUMB. xv. 24-29.

1.

SOME say he was a Teuton. Where the vine
    Purples the hillsides of his fatherland
Were bred those hinds, they say, beside the Rhine,
    Who toss'd the dice, with red remorseless hand,
On Jesu's raiment. These His corse divine
    Watch'd in the sepulchre; a brutal band
Pacing, stern sentries, round that sealèd tomb,
Their shimmering helmets glittering in the gloom.

2.

It may be so; the legend suits my song.
    With Pilate came they, those barbarians bold,
To make his weak dominion sternly strong
    And quell the tribes of Jacob in their hold;
Those tribes so fierce against the Romans' wrong,
    Untamed and turbulent and uncontroll'd,
And daring oft ev'n Roman chiefs to vex,
While Cæsar's yoke weigh'd heavy on their necks.

3.

With these, 'twas Pilate's task and toil austere
  To make Tiberius' mastery supreme ;
Nor marvel that with policy severe
  He scorned their superstitions as a dream.
Not worse than other Romans, his career
  Was cruel and remorseless in its scheme.
'Twas policy alike for Jew and Greek
To trample on the proud and spare the meek.

4.

A heathen ; but where Caiaphas was priest,
  And Judas an apostle, soft should be
A Christian's sad reproaches. This at least
  Concede to Pilate in the history
Of that portentous day, that bloody feast,
  When even apostles trembl'd and could flee :
Not all, perchance, ignoble was his mood,
Who strove and pleaded, feared, and yet withstood.

5.

Stern, tearless, of the earth so earthy all,
  Dragg'd from his rest at day-break, see him tread
Contemptuous o'er the marbles of his hall,
  Scorning the rabble that disturb'd his bed.
Fierce he goes forth, impatient at their call,
  And lo ! the Lamb, rope-bound and thief-like led,
'Mid priests and nobles with their motley crowd,
Meekly majestic stands, His forehead bowed.

6

6.

Grand in his awful goodness, lambkin dumb
  Before his shearers—how the satrap shrinks
From that dejected front, amid the hum
  Of voices claiming judgment. Courage sinks
Before his victim, as like fiends they come,
  Clinch'd fists uplifted, and strange tongues methinks,
Greek, Hebrew, Latin mingled. Hear their cry!
Can Pilate scruple one more Jew should die?

7.

Now opes the dreadful drama of that day!
  "Take him, and judge him for yourselves." He turns
As one contemptuous from their hordes away.
  Louder they clamour, he more fiercely spurns,
While thirsting for Messiah's blood they say—
  "Not ours to deal the shameful death he earns,
Who breaks our law; and then 'tis thine alone,
'Gainst Cæsar's rival, to uphold the throne."

8.

" He makes himself a king ! " they said. 'Twas meet
  The son of David, of that palace floor,
Should tread its art Mosaic under feet !
  There—never stood a Nazarene before ;
But Pilate leads him towards his judgment seat,
  And talks with him apart, where arching o'er

The glistening pavement, set with coloured stones,
Vaults flamed with gold, a glory meet for thrones.

9.

" Art *thou* a king, then ? " to the Lamb serene
His judge makes question ; while, instinct with fear,
His eye surveys that meek yet manly mien,
And feels 'tis strange that he should stand so near
The heir of Solomon. He hearkens keen :
"Thou sayest it—Who told it thee?" But hear—
More strange those words that followed, when, forsooth,
Of truth He spake! Said Pilate: "What is truth ?"

10.

Think of that moment, when, more bright than morn,
Light o'er that heathen flash'd, and left him dazed.
Echoes within his breast a thought new-born,
As on that awful sufferer he gazed :
Yes—" What is truth ?" he answered, not with scorn ;
From Truth incarnate, turning more amazed,
To speak God's truth, defiant of assault:
Hear him proclaim, "I find in him no fault."

11.

Comes to his ear, amid their wild uproar,
    Herod's foul name. Of guilt in Galilee,
They charge this man of Nazareth! Full sore
    The hate twixt him and Herod; yet, thought he,
This shall make peace between us twain once
    more.
I'll send the case to Herod for decree:
"Take him to Herod, then," if so ye say.
Frantic they hear and sullen they obey.

12.

Behold "that fox"! To his hyæna-den
    They drag the pallid Jesus. Bloody sweat,
And those long hours of wakefulness—and then
    His famishing and shiv'ring, why forget?
These have already marr'd this "scorn of men,"
    This patient Man of sorrows. Lo! 'tis set,
The court of Herod, and amid their bands,
Silent, while they make mirth, Messiah stands.

13.

"No answer and no miracle," exclaim
    The slaves of Herod; "let him give us sport."
Yes, "turn him o'er to spitting and to shame,"
    The tyrant bids. They mock his mute deport,
And men of war deride his regal fame:
    "Now, send him back to Pilate's meaner
    court,
And deck'd in robes of lustre he shall go,
Led forth with laughter, o'er his way of woe."

14.

Behold, once more 'round Pilate rings their call;
  Once more his pride confronts their rage, alas!
Peevish, far more than proud, and scorning all
  He sees or hears; for now the surging mass
Rages like stormy tides of mire and gall,
  Resentful, as they beg for Bar-Abbas.
" Not Jesus, but the robber!" so they cried.
" But, Jesus, then?"   " Let him be crucified!"

15.

Pilate, thy time has come, if man thou art,
  To show thy manhood once, if nevermore!
Nay, see him, baffled, feebly faint of heart,
  Of motives mix'd, as 'mid the mad uproar,
Trembles the balance and new fears upstart.
  One moment—while their clamour calls for gore—
He feels a conscience in his bosom beat;
And, silent, ponders on his judgment-seat.

16.

For Claudia's message meets him with her plea,
  Her dream of " that Just Man." And shall it win
Justice from such a spouse? Affrighted he—
  Nay, more affrighted—turns once more within,
To ask—" Whence art thou?" Awful mystery!
  They call'd him " Son of God " amid their din.
Yes—oh! " whence art thou?" What if so it were?
Could God more god-like meet a worshipper?

17.

As the weak wall resists and not the rock,
  So he withstands ; so smite in dread recoil
Those waves of fury. Hear their frightful mock—
  "Thou art not Cæsar's friend!" Their wild turmoil
Strikes at his master-passion, like the shock
  Of ocean, when its depths uprise and boil.
Once more, while yet their crafty cries they urge,
Pilate acquits—and gives Him to the scourge.

18.

Then cometh Jesus forth, in thorny crown
  And robe of purple purpled now afresh :
For streams the beaded blood his face adown ;
  And of his shoulders bleeds the furrow'd flesh.
Behold that diadem of Christ's renown ;
  No sheen of gold that glitters in the mesh
Shows like those thorns—withstand the sight, who can ?
So Pilate feels and cries,—" Behold the man !"

19.

Behold the Man : behold God's only Son !
  Pilate turns preacher : and who else, like him,
Before mankind hath set the Holy One ?
  So, seen of angels and the seraphim,
And seen of sinners thus, while Time shall run,
  Through dazzled eyes, which contrite tears bedim—
Behold the Lamb ! They see—and yet they cry,
" Away with Him ! Him let us crucify."

PONTIUS PILATE.   87

20.

Bring hither water and the laver bring !
  See Pilate wash his hands ; he deems 'tis fit
To them and to their seed this guilt should cling:
  "His blood on us shall be "—they echo it !
"His cross, at least, shall bear His claim of King :
  And mine the maxim—What is writ is writ."
" See, I am innocent of blood," he cries,
Uplifting his wash'd hands before their eyes.

21.

Mock not this rite baptismal : Who art thou
  Call'd Christian, but in spirit all unbless'd,
And oft ashamed of Jesus ?   On thy brow
  The cross is seal'd, but when with loyal breast
Hast thou for Him fulfilled the soldier's vow,
  Or for that thorny crown and purple vest
Stood forth like Pilate !   When hast thou, sore-tried,
Wash'd ev'n thine hands to own the Crucified."

22.

Take heed when Sodom's self at Christ's right hand,
  And foul Gomorrah plead before His bar,
Lest Pilate rise to judge thee, and may stand
  At that great day anear and thou afar :
Art thou Christ's soldier ?   'Mid the guilty band
  Of them that hate Him, hast thou gained one scar ?

Scoff not at Pilate's laver, self-baptized,
If less than his thy christ'ning hath sufficed.

23.

Yet can such guilt be pardon'd ! Who shall say?
   Faith may remove great mountains, and who knows
That Pilate ne'er repented ? But that day
   Full many a Christian Pilate shall disclose ;
And if that blood their sins can wash away,
   Who crucify afresh the Man of Woes,
Why not poor Pilate's ? Christ's atonement free,
Washeth all nations, like the vasty sea.

24.

Much have I ponder'd Pilate with such thought,
   Weighing His Word, whose ev'ry word is weigh'd,
And while I hope for him, presuming naught,
   'Tis mine own sin that makes my soul dismay'd,
Lest to the Christian's door the crime be brought
   While ev'n for Pilate pardon is up laid.
Before that day judge nothing : leave him there,
   With Him who for His murderers poured His prayer.

25.

Yet for all heathen in their vale of death
   Make broad this hope ; and think of Pilate then,

How day by day, as with all nations' breath,
   His name is named in all the tongues of men.
"Suffer'd by Pontius Pilate "—so it saith ;
   Nor is one human name within my ken
So frequent utter'd as this name unblest,
O'er all the lands and oceans, east or west.

26.

By men, by maids, by boys, by women all,
   And all their years of life 'tis said or sung.
Where the great Minster lifts its lofty wall,
   Who hath not heard its echoes, while the tongue
Upsends the Creed, before the people fall
   Upon their bended knees—the old and young ?
Ev'n at his mother's knee the babe must frame
With pouting lip to lisp poor Pilate's name.

27.

Sounds not the dread indictment too severe,
   Roll'd round the globe, and, like the wand'ring Jew,
Never let die ?   But—mercy's accents hear :
   "The princes of this world, they never knew
The wisdom that for Christians shines so clear,
   Else had they never done the deed—who slew
The Lord of Glory."   So exclaims St. Paul,
And let his verdict plead for Gentiles all.

28.

And ev'n at Pilate's bar, that bleeding Lamb
   Hear how His lips dropp'd mercy 'mid his foes:

" Not thine the greater sin." Nor Creed nor
 psalm
  Forbids the hopes that spring from words like
  those.
This of his great Atonement lifts the palm
  Victorious over Satan ! Still it flows
That fountain of Salvation ; still arise
The fuming savours of that sacrifice.

29.

Hear Peter plead : " My brethren : Well, I wot
  Through ignorance ye did it, as did they—
Your rulers : for ev'n Pilate faltered not,
  Determined to release him—nor gave way
Till ye denied the Just One." Ne'er forgot,
  Be what the Man of Tarsus too might say,
As for himself so for the world beside:
" Mercy I gain'd, for blindly I denied."

30.

Nor shall the rocks of Sinai with their flame
  Prevail against the Cross ; nor those dread
  seals
Against the Lamb that opes them. His blest
  claim
  The rainbow round His throne in light re-
  veals ;
And sure the heathen in Messiah's name
  May see Salvation. Ev'n the law appeals
For mercy to "the stranger," and makes room
For Gentiles, where its Hebrew censers fume.

31.

Yes, for "the stranger" are soft words engrav'd
    Deep in the law by Moses' iron pen :
For sins of ignorance the sin-enslaved
    Find mercy in the sweet Atonement then.
For oh ! the depth ! if Pilate may be saved,
    Sure there is pardon for the world of men,
And for all sinners grace is multiplied,
    Through the dear love of that blest Lamb that died.

32.

Methinks poor Pilate stands for human kind,
    For all who sin and know not what they do;
So tenderly did Jesus love the blind,
    So did His prayer ascend for them that slew.
Sure, where that crimson Cross hath never shined,
    Forgiveness may be found and glory too.
What Aaron's priest in type might waft away,
'Twas God's High-Priest wash'd out that dreadful day.

33.

Yes, worthy is the Lamb, and who shall tell
    How worthy, save His ransom'd there above,
Where those sweet Paschal anthems ever swell,
    And higher raptures in the angels move.
There they who drink from life's exhaustless well,
    And sing the wonders of redeeming love,

Shall show how mercy to the blind is given:
'Tis our presumptuous sins that cry to heaven !

34.

And this my comfort when I chant the Creed,
   That not for doom we name poor Pilate's name,
But, as it were, for guilty souls to plead,
   Who sin like him, unknown of sin the shame.
Oh ! blest be He who died to intercede,
   Methinks the depths of pardon we proclaim—
Naming one sinner's name, for whom He cried,
" Father, forgive them "—through the Crucified.

GABBATHA.

Ecce Homo.—S. John, xix. 5.

1.

The ploughers ploughed their furrows red
  Upon His back bent down,
Then, in the purple robe—His head
  Torn by the thorny crown—
Came forth of men the Man—and Pilate said:
    Behold the Man!

2.

The Man that is my fellow—saith
  God in the prophet's page:
Behold the Man of Nazareth
  Confronts the rabble's rage;
'Tis God-with-us consents to scorn and death.
    Behold the Man!

3.

He comes, He bleeds, and meek He stands,
  And mute His murderers gaze;
The reed bemocks His royal hands,
  Who God's own sceptre sways:
Bows ev'n the Roman heart that thus commands:
    Behold the Man!

4.

Oh ! moment in the march of time
   The greatest and the worst,
When stoops the Son of God sublime
   So low, 'mid men accurst.
'Tis heathen Pilate thus rebukes their crime :
     Behold the Man !

5.

Poor Pilate ! That stupendous scene
   He made, for oh ! he felt
How meek in Majesty His mien,
   And—sure their hearts must melt ;
So thought he—and he spake with awe, I ween:
     Behold the Man !

6.

Not then, as now, might instant Art
   That sight so dread make fast,
And grave, as with the sunbeam's dart,
   What they beheld aghast ;
But Lord ! of all mankind, make every heart
     Behold the Man !

7.

For nevermore shall fade away
   That momentary view ;
Age after age, day after day,
   To faithful souls made new:
Echoes that voice, and still shall sound for aye:
     Behold the Man !

8.

Nor yet that voice shall cease to thrill
  Ev'n those who sing the psalm
Of Moses on the heavenly hill ;
  For while they see the Lamb
And sing the Lamb once slain they hear it
    still :
      Behold the Man !

CALVARY.

In the Mount of the Lord it shall be seen.—GEN. xxii. 14.
In this Mountain.—ISAIAH, xxv. 6.

1.

As the strong swimmer spreads his hands to swim
    So shall his hands be spread,
And seen of angels, seen of seraphim
    Work wonders 'mid the dead ;
Shall spoil—of powers and princedoms of the air—
    Their portion and their prey,
Like Moses, when the Cross he made in prayer,
    On old Rephidim's Day.

2.

Here the dark veil of death that covers o'er
    The face of nations all,
Those pierced hands shall rend, and nevermore
    Their tears undried shall fall.
Death shall be swallowed up that day of days,
    In victory and peace ;
And in this mount of God shall songs of praise
    Begin, no more to cease.

3.

And there the Lord shall make our Paschal Feast ;
    Wines on the lees refined.

While swells the Alleluia, west and east,
    From all redeem'd mankind,
A man shall be our refuge from the storm,
    From blighting heat and shade ;
When for the poor oppress'd Immanuel's form
    The Crucified is made.
    7

FOLLOWING THE LAMB.

WHITHERSOEVER he goeth.—REV. xiv. 4.

1.

The patient Lamb of God, I see,
As forth He goes to Calvary,
And travels o'er that doleful road,
Bearing the cross, his bitter load.

2.

That cross, my soul, thy sins have made,
On Him thy sins that cross have laid:
How should the thought thy heart appall,
Beneath such load, to see Him fall!

3.

Oh, Lamb before Thy shearers dumb,
Like the Cyrenian lord I come,
And fain like him compelled would be,
To bear Thy burden after Thee.

4.

Let me for Thee take up the cross,
And count my life, my all, but loss,
If so partaker of Thy pain,
Thy crown at last may be my gain.

5.

Dear Lord, whatever cross it be
Thy love on earth allots to me,
Oh, may Thy servant ne'er repine,
Remembering what a cross was Thine !

6.

Yet make no sorer cross my share
Than Thou canst teach me how to bear ;
Remember, Lord, how frail I am,
How faint in following the Lamb !

THE CROSS-BEARER.

HIM they compelled to bear His cross.—ST. MATT. xxvii. 32.

1.

THE rustic Simon from Cyrene came,
    A Gentile born,
Perchance of Ham's dejected race and name,
    Who little dreamed that morn,
As to the town he fared to keep the Feast,
His name should be remember'd, west and east,
Forever and forever, as of one
Who did that day the deed which angels would have done.

2.

Him they compelled Messiah's cross to bear,
    With rude arrest ;
Mocking the plain wayfarer's vacant stare,
    His awe and look distress'd.
A stranger proselyte, amaz'd was he
Entangl'd in that rabble throng to be,
To hear the soldiers' cry and see withal
Beneath his cruel load the dear Redeemer fall.

3.

Unseen, what heavenly legions then down flew
    Him to upbear !
Archangels stretch'd their loving arms—but knew
    They might no further dare :
'Twas Simon's lot alone to lift the load,
And following Jesus o'er the tearful road,
To share his Saviour's burden : foremost he
Of all that bear the cross; who would not Simon be ?

4.

Who would not give his dearest Lord relief
    'Mid shame and blows ?
Who covets not to soothe the Saviour's grief
    With tender words, like those
Who follow'd near with woman's tears and cries ?
Nay, from such longings to life's duties rise :
Bear but the cross thou art compelled to bear,
And following thus thy Lord—so shalt thou do thy share.

THE WAY OF SORROWS.

Bearing His cross.—St. Luke.

1.

Bearing the cross, that baleful load,
He toils along the bitter road ;
The patient Lamb, the cruel tree
Drags forth to ghastly Calvary.

2.

When faint He falls, so worn and weak,
How to my soul His sorrows speak,
For in that load my sins I scan,
Borne by the lowly Son of Man.

3.

Soon was that cross His racking bed
For quivering limbs and writhing head,
Where streaming wound and straining eye
Told of His mortal agony.

4.

Blest Saviour, this for me to bear
Was thine, and what for Thee my share?
Shall I for Thee no prize lay down,
Accept no cross, yet claim the crown?

5.

Take up the cross! 'Tis hard to do,
But mercy comes with precept too:
Mine be the cross Thy love ordains,
What Christ compels His grace sustains.

GOLGOTHA.

And Abraham said, My son, God will provide Himself a Lamb.—Gen. xxii. 8.

1.

Little the rich man thought,
   When as that place of skulls, that field
Of frightful Golgotha he bought,
   All that he did was sealed
Long time before, in old Isaiah's song;
Strange what his gold might buy should not to him belong.

2.

It was Moriah's height,
   On the third day that did arise,
Marked by the dread Shekinah's light,
   To Father Abraham's eyes:
Fast by his side a youth pursued the road
Who on his shoulders bore a fagot's fearful load.

3.

" Here on this mount—God's hill,"
   The patriarch said, "it shall be seen—
Let us but work His holy will—
   What all these wonders mean."

"But where the Lamb?" the voice of Isaac
    cried:
"Here in this mount, my son, God will the Lamb
    provide."

4.

Lo! where the ram of old
    Was in the tangled thicket caught,
Where Isaac's bonds the cross foretold,
    That field the rich man bought.
In vile neglect Jehovah-Jireh lay;
And none remembered now that name of
    Abraham's day.

5.

The gibbet's baleful gloom,
    The jackal's loathsome feast was there,
Till Joseph made the rock a tomb
    And hedged a garden fair:
Nor dreamed that priests should seek, in Pilate's
    name,
That ransomed rock, once more, to rear a cross
    of shame.

6.

Isaiah's words fulfilled!
    On either hand a felon's tree,
For so the loving Father willed
    That His dear Son should be.
As with the wicked in his death of gloom,
So with the rich, in state, in faithful Joseph's
    tomb.

7.

That Golgotha accurst
   Holds the new Adam in its cave ;
And oh! how all unlike the first—
   An Eden from a grave
He gives in that sweet garden, where his Bride
Rose, like a fairer Eve, forth from his wounded
      side.

THE MAN OF SORROWS.

Is it nothing to you?—LAMENTATIONS, i. 12.

1.

THEY err not who have said, of yore,
Ev'n the child Jesus suffer'd sore,
And all His days for us the cross of Calvary bore.

2.

And Art this truth hath well made known,
Where—ev'n with Joseph's tools, is shown
The child who frames a cross to wake his mother's moan.

3.

Those lesser sorrows why forget,
That strewed the path before Him set,
And gathered 'round his death, as 'twere an evil net?

4.

He fasted in the desert bare;
But every day—behold His care
Of our indulgent flesh to taste no pleasing share.

5.

Those senses five that work our fall,
And oft the nobler mind enthrall,
How, in his passion's pangs, they suffered one and all!

6.

He saw—constrain'd His aching sight—
Men's faces fierce as beasts that fright,
Or made like shapes that scowl in visions of the
    night.

7.

He heard—as 'twere of fiends that fell—
The curses and the wolfish yell,
While murd'rers gnash'd their teeth and howl'd
    like hounds of hell.

8.

He smell'd—the savour foul and rank,
Ere gall and vinegar he drank;
And spittle smear'd his face from mouths like
    tombs that stank.

9.

He tasted—while they mock'd and laugh'd—
The dripping sponge, but left unquaff'd,
Ev'n in his thirst of death, that nauseous dole and
    draught.

10.

He felt—the blows, the thorns—but this
More keen than nails—the serpent-hiss
Of him who stung his cheek with treacherous lip
    and kiss.

11.

"Ye that pass by—behold and see,
The sorrows that are done to me.
And is it naught to you?" He asks—and answer
　　ye.

12.

We answer at the font, and there
Promise for His dear sake the cross to bear;
But, oh! forgive us Lord, and us poor sinners
　　spare.

THE CROSS.

<small>AND I, if I be lifted up from the earth, will draw all men unto me.—ST. JOHN, xii. 32.</small>

1.

SAVIOUR, on thine uplifted Tree
  How soon Thy saving work began,
Drawing all human hearts to Thee,
  For dying men the dying Man.

2.

Foremost of those who fled—draws near,
  With Mary by the cross to stand,
That one whom Jesus loved—to hear
  His pard'ning word, His sweet command.

3.

Full soon is changed the vacant stare
  Of those who raised the cross so high,
For sitting down they watched Him there,
  Touched by that meek, forgiving cry.

4.

Then scribe and priest the ebb discerned
  Of passion's tides that stormed before ;
When smote their breasts and slow returned
  Mockers who now could mock no more.

5.

Vain those appeals and scoffs renew'd—
  " Others He saved, not self, we see ; "

For conscience owns ingratitude ;
  So base ourselves, so gracious He !

6.

And lo ! the thief reclaimed at last
  Seems tow'rds the Christ more near to move,
For ev'n those arms, though pinioned fast,
  Embrace His all-embracing love.

7.

'Tis finished ! At the mighty cry
  Uprose the dark that veiled His death,
Forth flames the cross, in victory,
  While rend the flinty rocks beneath.

8.

Then broke one Roman heart as hard,
  That long had pondered with amaze,
And marvelled at the victim marr'd,
  That fixed his stern, astonish'd gaze.

9.

The moment that his Saviour died,
  Fresh from that heart came forth his creed:
" This was a righteous man," he cried—
  " This was the Son of God, indeed."

10.

O Lamb of God—that cross of thine,
  When shall mankind its glory see ?
When shall be felt its might divine,
  To draw all human hearts to Thee ?

THE THREE CROSSES.

HE said unto Jesus, Lord, remember me, when Thou comest into Thy kingdom.—ST. LUKE, xxiii. 42.

1.

AT morn or eve, one shining sphere
  Sheds its reflected light serene,
But holds its course the sun so near,
  That few the little star have seen.

2.

Behold in all its solar blaze
  The Cross of Christ, the death divine!
How mean beside its morning rays
  The martyr's noblest trophies shine!

3.

The thief's repentant cross to view
  Not many for a moment turn:
The Cross of Christ so near—how few
  Those meaner splendors can discern!

4.

Yet think what ev'n that cross supplies,
  And what reflected light it throws:
How the Great Cross it glorifies,
  And all its might and mercy shows!

THE THREE CROSSES.

5.

Not the mere martyr Jesus hangs
    Upon the nails and bows his head;
For His are our redemption's pangs,
    His blood is for atonement shed.

6.

That other cross the Saviour's power
    Displays in all His might to save;
He dies, but in that awful hour
    From Satan's thralldom frees the slave.

7.

Nor frees alone, but clothes with light
    The soul so dark to Him that turns:
For when were faith and hope more bright
    Than His, who there his God discerns?

8.

A king—though like a worm he seems;
    Almighty—though they crucify;
His God—though Him the priest blasphemes;
    His Saviour—who consents to die!

9.

The Resurrection and the Life,
    While groaning on the cross he hung;
How strong the faith, with fact at strife,
    That fired the malefactor's tongue!

10.

A thief, a sinner base at morn,
  On that blest Lamb has fix'd his eyes,
And heard His words—till, newly born,
  He lives—and all in glory dies.

11.

Dies, but confesses, first, his Lord;
  Pleads with his twin in shame and crime;
Repents and prays, and wins the word
  Of peace and promise so sublime.

12.

The faith that prayed—" Remember Me
  When Thou shalt in Thy kingdom come "—
How great! His kingdom to foresee;
  That Lamb before His shearers dumb!

13.

Back to fair Eden's guarded door
  Redeeming love in mercy goes;
The flaming sword is seen no more,
  Of Paradise the gates unclose.

14.

Of Paradise—but not the same,
  Nor of a kingdom far away;
But " thou, with me, who own'st my Name,
  Shalt be in Paradise this day."

15.

Thus dies the Christ, the war to wage
   With hosts of hell ; while yet to prove
His power to save—behold the gauge
   In this the trophy of His love !

16.

The earth its depth, the heaven its height,
   Its breadth the widespread world may know,
And lo ! the fourfold cross, in light,
   This parable might seem to show.

17.

Of Golgotha—those crosses three,
   That Cross of Christ, the twain between,
Unfold Redemption's mystery,
   And tell what all life's myst'ries mean.

18.

He that believes, though dead he were,
   Shall in His kingdom live and reign ;
Who scorns the Atoning Sufferer,
   Beholds His crimson'd cross in vain.

THE ATONEMENT.

No man may deliver his brother nor make agreement unto God for him, for it cost more to redeem their souls.— Ps. xlix. 7, 8.

1.

Hail Cross of Christ, whose crimson stains
Flow from the dear Redeemer's veins;
Our only hope, our only plea,
Our refuge from the storm is He;
And blest the Father's love, who gave—
In Him—the Mighty One to save.

2.

Of sinful flesh how poor the dream
That man his brother may redeem,
Or for himself redemption win,
By human merit cleansed from sin.
Dear Lamb of God, thy blood alone
Is all-sufficient to atone.

3.

Hail Cross of Christ, o'er life's dark sea,
Rising our Star of Hope to be!
Through clouds and storms that lower around
Thy radiance breaks, and peace is found,
And guided by thy light, at last,
The port appears, the waves are passed.

4.

Poor pilgrim through a world of woe,
While here I fare and toil below,
Cheer'd by thy beams, as pilgrims are
Who but descry one friendly star,
Still shall my heart contented sing,
Hail Cross of Christ, my God and King!

HYSSOP.

Purge me with hyssop and I shall be clean.—Psalm, li. 7.

1.

The bitter hyssop, springing from the wall,
  While Solomon the king is passing by,
  Of that imperial sage attracts the eye;
But did that eye foresee the vinegar and gall?

2.

A greater King than Solomon is here,
  Of that strange herb, the true interpreter,
  Whose pungent scent is as the bitter myrrh,
Whose taste like Sodom's sea, or Marah's fount austere.

3.

O'er Moses' book its spray the hyssop throws;
  Its crimson stain the Hebrew's door makes sure;
  The purge of sin, the loathsome leper's cure,
All teach—from Christ alone the blood of sprinkling flows.

4.

The awful groan from His deep heart that burst
  When, uncomplaining on the nails He hung,
  When, from the dust of death, His parchèd tongue
The last fierce torture told in that one word—I thirst:

5.

That cry expounds the Levite's hyssop-bough,
  The sponge, with gall and acrid juice, that drips,
  The reed with hyssop bound that mocks his lips—
All these, Messiah's signs, are seen in Jesus now.

6.

Kneel we beneath His Cross of Sacrifice,
  Smiting the breast, and trembling to draw near;
  Yet all these tokens reading, with deep fear,
While Nature blackens o'er: the Lord of Nature dies.

7.

For so, in jot and tittle, all fulfill'd,
  Even to the hyssop are His signs foreshown;
  Behold the piercèd side, th' unbroken bone;
The Paschal Lamb with bitter herbs is killed.

8.

Around the cross, with thorn and spear and reed,
  This plant we twine, of mystic worth not least;
  Behold and see, how for Our Great High Priest,
The Law and Prophets blend, to deck those hands that bleed!

THE DESIRE OF NATIONS.

So shall He sprinkle many nations.—ISAIAH, lii. 15.

1.

SAVIOUR, sprinkle many nations !
    Fruitful let thy sorrows be,
By thy pains and consolations
    Draw the Gentiles unto thee.
Of thy Cross the wondrous story,
    Be it to the nations told :
Let them see Thee in thy glory,
    And thy mercy manifold.

2.

Far and wide, though all unknowing,
    Pants for thee each mortal breast :
Human tears for Thee are flowing,
    Human hearts in Thee would rest.
Thirsting as for dews of even,
    Or the new-mown grass for rain,
Thee they seek as God of Heaven,
    Thee as man for sinners slain.

3.

Saviour, lo ! the isles are waiting,
    Stretched the hand and strained the sight,

For thy spirit, new-creating,
   Love's pure flame and wisdom's light :
Give the word, and of the preacher
   Speed the foot and touch the tongue,
Till on earth, by every creature,
   Glory to the Lamb be sung.

NICODEMUS.

WITH the rich in his death.—ISAIAH, liii., 9.

1.

THEY came to Nicodemus, him to mock
  Because with them no part he bore,
  And they had mock'd him once before :
Now let him share the shame and feel its shock !

2.

Him then they told his prophet was no more ;
  Was hanging lifeless on the tree ;
  With thieves was hanging—there on Calvary,
Just as the serpent was uphung of yore !

3.

Started that ruler at the taunt severe :
  Nay, have they made his blood to stream ?
  Made that white Lamb a serpent seem ?
Oh ! where was I ? Alas ! too late I hear.

4.

Came back those words—came back that lamp-
    lit scene,
  When first he sought the Christ to see,
  And came by night so stealthily,
'Mid Olive's groves to find the Nazarene :

5.

"As Moses lifted up that brazen sign,
  So must the Son of Man," he said,
  "Be lifted up." Strange words and dread!
But now 'tis all unveil'd—their sense divine.

6.

Uprose that ruler of the Jews: uprose
  Unwonted courage in his breast.
  He came with Joseph, and thrice blest
These bore the dear Redeemer to repose.

THE BURIAL.

THEN took they the body of Jesus and wound it in linen clothes, with the spices as the manner of the Jews is to bury. ST. JOHN, xix., 40.

1.

YES, 'tis finished ! All is done
Man could do to God the Son.
Hangs He there upon the Tree ;
In His side the Fountain see,
Gory hands and drooping brow,
Bruised and marr'd ! 'Tis finished now.

2.

Loose we then the thorny crown ;
Take the glorious victim down ;
Draw the nails with tender care ;
Gently, now, the body bear:
Spread and fold his winding-sheet,
Store its bands with spices sweet.

3.

Through the garden, seek the tomb;
Lift the torch to light its gloom ;
Lo ! about the sacred bier
Prince and senator appear !
With the poor his dwellings were
With the rich his sepulchre !

4.

Roll the stone upon the door!
Longing, looking back once more,
Turn we as we beat the breast,
Leaving Jesus to His rest.
Gentle Marys, do not stay;
Hallow yet one Sabbath-day!

THE SEPULCHRE.

To the mountain of myrrh and to the hill of frankincense, until the day break and the shadows flee away.—CANTICLES, iv., 6.

1.

YE that, lingering near the spot,
Keep your vigil fearing not ;
Musing, weeping, where the grave
Holds the guest that died to save.

2.

Holy Marys—saw ye then,
How they came with armèd men ?
Heard, as through a wilderness,
Heavy footsteps near you press ?

3.

" Whose the tomb ? For whom ? " they cry,
As their torches blaze on high;
"Come we, lest the dead should stir—
Sentries round a sepulchre ? "

4.

Tell them 'tis the royal bed
Where a conqueror lays his head :
'Tis the rest of David's son ;
'Tis the couch of Solomon !

5.

By these signs of pillar'd smoke,
Learn of what the prophet spoke ;
For the funeral lights ye bear,
Fume with spice and incense rare.

6.

Let the glorious Victor sleep,
Threescore guards his state shall keep,
Posted round, a goodly sight,
Sword on thigh, through all the night.

7.

Roman guards, expert in war,
Israel's too, not less ye are :
If—" no king but Cæsar "—then,
Ye are Israel's valiant men !

8.

Jealous Jews, that slew your King,
Lo ! what royal pomp ye bring,
Guilty fears may thus provide
Honours for the Crucified.

9.

Shines the moon—the guard is set ;
Glistening helms with dew-drops wet,
And their spears make shining show,
Pacing slowly to and fro.

10.

Seal the stone with Pilate's gem ;
Daughters of Jerusalem,
By the hinds and by the roes
Rouse him not from sweet repose.

11.

Where the mountain scents of myrrh,
Frankincense and fragrant fir,
He is gone, till break of day,
Till the shadows flee away.

12.

He that in the garden knelt,
He in Olive's groves that dwelt,
Here His bruisèd flesh hath laid,
In a garden's grateful shade.

13.

Leave Him—'tis the prophet's word—
Till the turtle's voice is heard ;
Leave Him till the darkness flees :
Wake Him not until He please.

EASTER.

THE Lion of the tribe of Judah, the Root of David, hath prevailed.—REV. v., 5.

1.

WAKE the world! The morning breaks,
Lo! the Lord of life awakes,
See his glory in the skies!
Christ is risen: let us rise.
Of His Promise naught hath failed:
Judah's Lion hath prevailed.

2.

Sing the patient Lamb's repose,
Sing the Lion that uprose:
Lamb of God, our sins to bear,
Lion, death and hell to tear;
Lamb-like in the grave to lie;
Judah's Lion ne'er to die.

3.

Wake, the wondrous tale to tell
How He broke the bars of hell.
He that lay among the dead,
Death itself hath captive led:
Death and hell, the sting and flame,
Judah's Lion overcame.

4.

Wake the never-ending psalm ;
Song of Moses and the Lamb ;
Of the Lamb, a Victim rent,
Of the Lion's hardiment,
Spread His praise from shore to shore :
Judah's Lion dies no more.

5.

Sing His waking from the dead ;
Shook the hills, the ocean fled :
Springs of life the grave revealed,
Garden closed and fountain sealed ;
And, like lightning from the gloom,
Judah's Lion rent the tomb.

6.

Christ is risen ! weep no more :
Sing the glorious Conqueror ;
Songs of His salvation sing :
Where, O Death, thy cruel sting !
Worthy is the Lamb once slain ;
Judah's Lion, live and reign !

EASTER IN THE GARDEN.

VERY early in the morning, the first day of the week, they came unto the Sepulchre at the rising of the sun.—ST. MARK, xvi., 2.

MARY AND SALOME.

TELL us, Gard'ner dost thou know
Where the Rose and Lily grow,
Sharon's Crimson Rose and pale
Judah's Lily of the Vale?
Rude is yet the opening year,
Yet their sweetest breath is here.

GARDENER.

Daughters of Jerusalem,
Yes, 'tis here we planted them,
'Twas a Rose all red with gore,
Wondrous were the thorns it bore!
'Twas a body swathed in white,
Ne'er was Lily half so bright.

THE WOMEN.

Gentle Gard'ner, even so,
What we seek thou seem'st to know.
Bearing spices and perfume,
We are come to Joseph's tomb;
Breaks ev'n now the rosy day;
Roll us, then, the stone away.

GARDENER.

Holy women! this the spot.
Seek Him, but it holds Him not.
This the holy mount of myrrh,
Here the hills of incense were,
Here the bed of His repose,
Till, ere dawn of day, He rose.

MAGDALENE.

Yes, my name is Magdalene:
I myself the Lord have seen.
Here I came, but now, and wept
Where I deem'd my Saviour slept.
But He called my name—and lo!
Jesus lives, 't is even so.

GARDENER.

Yes, the mountains skipped like rams;
Leaped the little hills like lambs.
All was dark, when shook the ground,
Quaked the Roman soldiers round,
Streamed a glorious light, and then
Lived the Crucified again.

THE WOMEN.

Magdalene hath seen and heard!
Gard'ner, we believe thy word.
But oh! where is Jesus fled,
Living and no longer dead?
Tell us, that we too may go
Where the Rose and Lily grow.

MAGDALENE.

Come, the stone is rolled away ;
See the place where Jesus lay ;
See the lawn that wrapp'd His brow ;
Here the angel sat but now.
"Seek not here the Christ," he said ;
"Seek not life among the dead."

ALL.

Seek we then the life above ;
Seek we Christ, our Light and Love.
Now His words we call to mind :
If we seek Him we shall find ;
If we love Him we shall go
Where the Rose and Lily grow.

THE EASTER EUCHARIST.

He was known of them in breaking of bread.—St. Luke, xxiv., 35.

1.

Body of Jesus, oh sweet food !
Blood of my Saviour, precious Blood !
On these thy gifts, Eternal Priest,
Grant Thou my soul in faith to feast.

2.

Weary and faint I thirst and pine
For Thee my Bread, for Thee my Wine,
Till strengthen'd—as Elijah trod,
I journey to the Mount of God.

3.

There, clad in white, with crown and palm,
At the great supper of the Lamb,
Be mine, with all thy Saints to rest,
Like him that leaned upon thy breast.

4.

Saviour, till then, I fain would know
That feast above by this below ;
This Bread of Life, this wondrous Food,
Thy Body and Thy precious Blood.

THE BIRD SONG.

THE flowers appear on the earth, the time of the singing of birds is come, and the voice of the turtle is heard in our land.
—CANTICLES, ii., 12.

1.

THE winter is over and gone at last,
The days of snow and rain are past,
Over the fields the flowers appear,
It is the Turtle's voice we hear.

CHORUS.

The singing of birds,
A warbling band,
And the Spirit's voice!
The voice of the Turtle is heard in our land.

REPEAT.—The time it is of the singing of birds,
The singing of birds, etc.

2.

And gone are the plaintive days of Lent,
The week of the Cross with Christ we spent.
Now he giveth us joy for woe—
Gather the flowers the first that blow.

CHORUS.

The singing of birds,
A warbling band,
And flowers are words,
Are words the faithful may understand.

REPEAT.—The time it is, etc.

3.

A sepulchre sealed, a rock its door,
But winter is gone and comes no more.
The seal is broken, and now are seen
Valleys and woods and gardens green !

CHORUS.

The singing of birds,
A warbling band,
'Mid flocks and herds
The song of all Nature is heard in our land !

REPEAT.—The time it is, etc.

4.

And Christ is the song of everything !
For Death is winter, and Christ the spring ;
Fountains that warble in purling words—
Hark ! how they echo the " Song of Birds : "

CHORUS.

The singing of birds,
A warbling band,
And the purling words
Of brooks and waters are heard in our land.

REPEAT.—The time it is of the singing of birds,
The singing of birds,
A warbling band,
And the Spirit's voice !
The voice of the Turtle is heard in our land.

THE BUTTERFLY.

I have said to corruption thou art my father; to the worm thou art my mother and my sister.—Job, xvii., 14.

1.

Where the grave-digger plies his fearful trade,
    With mattock and with spade,
Upturning bones and skulls of hollow eye,
Oft lights upon a head, the butterfly,
Cresting its forehead with a gaudy wing,
And fluttering, like a soul, about that horrid thing.

2.

An idle thought; but, in that garden's bound,
    That place of skulls around,
Hovered, perchance, that day the Saviour rose,
The Tyrian moth, as beautiful as those
Whose purpled pinions glitter in the sun
Of Ormuz or of Ind, arrayed like Solomon.

3.

Nor deem it vain, a worm may seem sublime
    In Easter's golden prime,
Thus deck'd, and flitting like embodied breath
That pants in resurrection out of death,
For thus to me a parable is shown;
What Christ of lilies spake expounds not flowers alone.

4.

For if a worm in winding-sheet down lies,
    Instinct with power to rise ;
If the poor thing that crawled may soar—a
    nymph,
That fed on dust—may suck the honey'd lymph,
That rotted in dishonour—may be seen
Transfigur'd ev'n like him that dazzled Sheba's
    Queen.

5.

Oh ! faithless we, shall God so clothe a worm,
    So raise from earth that form,
And leave His children dear, in icy shade,
All unremember'd and forgotton laid ?
Shall we, when Christ returns, less glorious
    spring
Out of the dust of death than that transfigur'd
    thing ?

EASTER-EGGS.

My hand hath found, as a nest, the riches of the people, and as one gathereth eggs.—ISAIAH x. 14.

1.

My godson, dear delighted child,
Held up his Easter-eggs, and wild
  With Easter-mirth, ranged here and there,
To show their colours, manifold,
Their dappled hues, their blue and gold,
  Like mossy agates rich and rare.

2.

Nonsense profane for Easter day,
Away with toys—the churl might say:
  But nay, dear boy, hear words of mine!
These colours kindly Art hath made;
But hidden in the forest's shade,
  The birds have brighter eggs than thine.

3.

Where thickest hazels weave a screen,
The school-boy prying through the green,
  When blossoms first the fragrant May,
Spies, deep the tangled boughs amid,
The mother-bird, in nest half-hid,
  Till—there, alas! she whirrs away.

4.

He gazes—but he scorns a theft :
What pebbles in her nest she left,
   What marvels and what wondrous dyes !
How strange, beneath a warbler's wings,
That God should hide such mystic things
   From man's cold heart and faithless eyes.

5.

Night's glitt'ring worlds the Maker plann'd,
Yet deigned the same Almighty hand
   To deck the little linnet's nest,
And freak with many a brilliant boss,
Those pearls, within their bed of moss,
   She presses with maternal breast.

6.

Then let the precious gems lie hid ;
For so thy mother, boy, would bid,
   She that hath made thy bed so soft ;
Yet come thou mayest, to watch the spot,
Till forth from each enamell'd grot,
   Breaks life, at last, and springs aloft.

7.

Heavenward it soars, and soaring, sings
An Easter-song, on joyous wings,
   For lo ! what seem'd a stone is rent ;
Like Joseph's sepulchre it breaks ;
Forth springs a living thing, and wakes
   Each list'ning ear to ravishment.

8.

There's not a wing that cleaves the sky
But once did, like the Saviour, lie
   All seal'd, as in a stony grave.
These creatures scarce to earth belong ;
They fill the firmament with song ;
   They sing the Lamb that died to save.

9.

The Resurrection and the Life
Well may their nests, with myst'ry rife
   To man's dull soul and sense portend.
So, when Christ's coming gilds its gloom,
Shall break the torpor of the tomb ;
   So, shall the sons of God ascend.

10.

And such the sympathy, they say,
Of birds with Christ, on Easter-Day,
   When from His rocky tomb He sprung,
That every egg, in every nest
Of Golgotha, gave forth its guest,
   And with their songs the garden rung.

11.

As seeds to flowers, so eggs had turn'd
To brilliant things the earth that spurn'd,
   And sought the skies on gladsome wing :
Birds of all plumages, 'tis said,
Sung—Christ is risen from the dead,
   And taught us Easter-hymns to sing.

12.

And so, where Carmel's lily grows,
Where wafts the scent of Sharon's rose,
   Where warbles sweet Siloah's rill,
The pilgrim, at the Paschal-tide,
May hear, with many a song beside,
   The turtle's voice of rapture still.

13.

Then marvel not, where mystery lies
Of life in eggs, that God most wise
   Disdains not, thus, to bid us learn ;
Teaching alike the boy and man
By faith fond Nature's lore to scan,
   With childlike hearts within that burn.

14.

So she, the Second Adam's Bride,
That rose like Eve from Jesu's side,
   Of Him " who dwells in gardens " sings,
And still in gardens hears His voice,
Where birds, at Easter-tide rejoice,
   And every nest breaks forth and sings.

THE ROYAL YARN.

1. BIND this line of scarlet thread in the window.—JOSHUA. ii. 18.

2. Take cedar-wood, scarlet, and hyssop.—LEVIT. xiv. 4.

3. He took blood and water, and scarlet wool, and hyssop.—HEB. ix. 19.

1.

SHONE the sun, that Easter-Monday,
  O'er the new-grown grass and green,
O'er the pleasant slopes of Greenwich
  And the sports that there were seen:
But, while youth around me frolicked
  In that holiday of Spring,
Sat I by an ancient sailor,
  With the sailor gossiping.

2.

Told he me how, under Nelson,
  From the Indies to the Nile,
Served he, till at fierce Trafalgar,
  He had seen his dying smile:
How he whisper'd—" Kiss me, Hardy,"
  How in death he laid him down:
But he sigh'd that such a hero
  Fought not under Jesu's Crown.

3.

Changed his gossip as I questioned
   How his sailor-life, so free,
Him had made so good a Christian :
   " 'Twas the royal yarn," quoth he.
" Through my life, that thread is woven ;
   With my christ'ning it began ;
Everywhere, that kingly token
   Marks my story, boy and man."

4.

" Now, you know," quoth he, " good Master,
   How the royal yarn is sign
That the Crown claims all that bears it,
   Canvass, cordage, rope, and twine ;
So, one time, I heard the parson
   Say, by Faith we might discern
Woven in our life and fortunes
   Christ our Saviour's royal yarn :"

5.

" How we are His Crown's possession,
   Marked for Him ; and by this clue
We may trace His grace and goodness
   Running all our lifetime through.
What the parson preach'd I thought of "—
   So the sailor's tale ran on,
" When off Moro-Castle lying,
   Sick I lay and well nigh gone."

6.

"For the royal yarn was woven
   In my hammock as I swung,
And my conscience saw another
   All my threads of life among :
So upon my weary pallet,
   As I turn'd and thought it o'er,
Swore I, to Christ's Crown forever
   I'd be faithful, ship and shore."

7.

Prosed yet more that ancient sailor,
   But no more his yarn I heard :
For another thought had started
   In my spirit, at his word :
For that sign of Crown-possession,
   And that thread of royal hue
Gave me insight of the Scriptures ;
   Gave me to its types a clue.

8.

Of the Royal line of Judah,
   See what scarlet symbols show ;
See how, like the weaver's shuttle,
   Prophets thread them to and fro ;
How, on Zarah's wrist withdrawing,
   Scarlet mark'd redemption's claim ;
How, in Rahab's window glowing,
   'Twas Messiah's royal Name.

9.

So the scarlet wool of Moses
    Did the scarlet robe foretell,
So, proclaiming—*Ecce Homo*,
    Jesus King of Israel,
Through the symbols of His passion
    Scourges, thorns, and scoffs amid,
Weaves this one Imperial token,
    Gleaming forth, or deftly hid.

10.

And the Bride, with lips of scarlet,
    Thus expounds the mystic Word,
Where with hyssop, and with cedar,
    Scarlet binds the living bird;
Where, through all the Scriptures woven,
    Bright this royal yarn is seen,
Everywhere Messiah's token,
    Token of the Nazarene.

EASTER VIRELAY.

Wake thou that sleepest and arise from the dead and Christ shall give thee light.—Ephesians, v. 14.

1.

Wake thou that sleepest!
Joy thou that weepest,
  Lift up the head!
Cease from thy moaning
Sighing and groaning,
  Rise from the dead.

2.

Weary wayfarer,
Fainting cross-bearer,
  Bending adown;
Hark! how the Spirit
Bids thee inherit
  Life and a crown.

3.

Lo! to restore thee
Christ goes before thee,
  Through the deep vale,
Gloomy and darkling;
Paradise sparkling
  There shall unveil.

4.

Flee to the mountain!
There, find the fountain;
    Wash and be white.
Joy thou that weepest,
Wake thou that sleepest,
    Christ gives thee light.

SONG FOR EASTER.

BREAK forth into singing.—ISAIAH.

1.

CHRIST hath arisen!
Broken His prison,
  Man to deliver
    From death's gloomy reign.
Victor Immortal!
Hell's gloomy portal
  Of brass and of iron
    He rendeth in twain.

2.

Wake every nation!
Songs of salvation
  Round the great earth
    Let them echo to-day.
Life to the dying!
Sorrow and sighing
  The sunrise of glory
    Hath driven away.

3.

Darkness hath vanished!
Death's sting is banished:
  See the bright mansions
    Of Paradise ope!

Grave thou art broken;
Jesus hath spoken
  Joy to the Universe,
  Glory and Hope.

4.

Tell how He liveth :
Sing what He giveth ;
  Sound the great name
  Of the risen I-AM
Feed on His manna :
Raise the Hosanna !
  Full be the choral-song
  Worthy the Lamb.

EASTER IN PATMOS.

I was in the Spirit on the day of the Lord.—Revelation, i. 10.

1.

'Twas on the day the Lord had made,
    The day that rent his rocky tomb,
St. John in lonely Patmos strayed,
    While glorious, as from ocean's womb,
Arose the sun—and lo! there came
    A trumpet voice; the exile turned,
And One whose eyes were fiery flame
He saw—the Word of God His Name,
    Where sevenfold lights about him burned.

2.

In rapture, by that sea-girt shore,
    He Jesus sees, whom Jesus loved,
Who was and is forevermore,
    Faithful and true His promise proved.
Breathes from his lips the Spirit's sword,
    Shines from his face the noon-tide sun;
Of death and hell the mighty Lord,
His are the keys and His the Word
    Of Life—the everlasting One.

3.

A voice of many waters—His,
    Who liveth and was dead the while;

He opes the seven-seal'd book, and this
  Is Easter in that holy isle :
A vision of the Lamb and throne,
  Of Judah's Lion and His might,
Worthy to loose the seals alone,
And all the Church's way make known,
  Through death and darkness into light.

4.

The Paschal hymns of heaven are heard,
  The Lamb that once was slain, their song—
From numbers without numbers stirred,
  Response with rapture to prolong.
I read and lo ! I seem to hear
  From great creation's dawn and end,
From earth and sky and every sphere,
One Alleluia broad and clear,
  From all the sons of God ascend.

5.

Day of the Lord, of year or week,
  Whene'er it shines a Paschal Feast,
On that blest day His flock to seek
  The Shepherd comes, our Great High Priest;
Comes to our sins a flame of fire,
  Comes to our faith like Gilead's balm,
Comes to our love and fond desire,
And joins us to the heavenly choir
  In that eternal Paschal Psalm.

6.

He comes, our prophet, priest and king,
  That Alpha and Omega scroll
To open, and what Time shall bring—
  Age upon ages—to unroll.
Of earth and heaven the keynote words
  He gives His suffering saints to guide,
Till ceaseth din of spears and swords,
Till King of kings and Lord of lords,
  He comes again to crown His Bride.

7.

Descends the New Jerusalem ;
  He reigns who maketh all things new ;
The Church in sparkling diadem,
  In white those virgin souls we view.
The sea of glass, so bright and calm,
  Glitters the rainbow'd throne before,
And sounds th' eternal Paschal Psalm,
That song of Moses and the Lamb,
  With Alleluias, evermore.

THE ANGELS ON THE ARK.

> To the intent that now unto the principalities and powers in heavenly places might be known by the Church, etc.—EPHESIANS, iii. 10.

1.

THE cherubim o'ershadowing the Ark
   Looked down upon the mercy-seat that shone,
And covered o'er the Law profoundly dark,
   Those tables twain by Moses hewn of stone;
   That writing of no hand save God's alone,
That was against us—flaming red,
Like Tekel on the wall so dread,
To poor Belshazzar's ear that was interpreted.

2.

What things those cherubs seemed intent to scan
   The same all angels scan with awe to-day;
The Law's dire curse, condemning sinful man,
   By mercy covered—ta'en by it away.
   And oh, the depth! still, oh! the depth—they say:
The depth and height and breadth sublime
Of Jesu's mercy covering crime,
Of Christ, the only Ark, the Word made flesh in time.

3.

Bring forth the deaf with ears that will not hear,
   Bring forth the blind with eyes that will not see

What wondrous things are in that Law austere,
  Beneath that golden lid enshrined that be,
  Where the Shekinah shines eternally.
Behold ! the Ark, God's glorious Son,
Th' atoning Lamb, the Holy One,
That takes away our sins : He bleeds and it is done.

4.

Lo ! when on earth, responsive to the skies,
  Uprises like a cloud upon the gale,
The incense of our Easter sacrifice,
  When the pure altar's mysteries unveil,
  And high Trisagion thrills our spirits frail,
In holy awe and thought intent,
I seem to see all heaven down bent,
To learn from saints below new songs of ravishment.

5.

New songs, which none but pardon'd sinners know ;
  Love which the much forgiven alone can feel ;
The love of Christ to heirs of sin and woe;
  These to the height of heaven our deeds reveal.
  The chariots of God, on burning wheel,
Pause in full course our hymns to hear ;
Legions of angels bow their ear,
And through the Church on earth they draw to God more near.

RHODA.

A DAMSEL named Rose.—Acts, xii. 13.

1.

SWEET Paschal Rose, thy fragrant name
Blossoms in all the golden flame
    Of that blest Easter Morn,
When Peter, from the bonds abhorr'd
Of Herod and his threatened sword,
Rose glorious, like His risen Lord,
    To light and life new-born.

2.

Dark was the Paschal Eve, that year,
When met the trembling saints in fear,
    All night for him to pray.
The great apostle, doom'd to die,
Though soaring where the angels fly,
Must leave the flock forlorn to sigh,
    Ev'n on an Easter-Day.

3.

Meanwhile, in prison-bonds he slept,
Peaceful—yet dreaming that he wept
    Once more his shameful fall:
" Dear Master," in his dream, said he,
" My oath, at last, redeemed shall be;
In chains and death I follow Thee;
    My sin—forgive it all ! "

RHODA. 157

4.

Again, the crowing cock he hears,
And flow afresh those bitter tears :
  But—does he wake or sleep ?
Like Lot's, his hand an angel takes :
From hands and feet the chains he shakes,
Bars fall and every barrier breaks—
  " Go, Peter ! feed my sheep."

5.

The guards are passed, strong gates unfold,
He breathes sweet air ! A morn of gold
  Reddens the eastern skies.
From death's dark dungeon of the night,
A parable of Jesus' might,
He rises into life and light,
  As all the saints shall rise.

6.

'Tis Easter ; and while yet 'tis dark,
The faithful, like the soaring lark,
  Have changed to praise their prayer :
At Mary's gate is heard a knock !
And Rhoda hastes to loose its lock—
When oh ! what voice, with wonder's shock,
  Sounds on her startled ear !

7.

Affrighted child she backward hies :
" 'Tis Cephas at the door," she cries,
  While still he knocks and waits :

His angel ?   Nay, himself !   'Tis he :
The Lord hath set his pris'ner free !
Once more the Church his face shall see !
　　Go haste, unbar the gates !

8.

Sweet Rose, of Easter flowers the first,
So did that Paschal morning burst
　　On thine elected sight !
Damsel august, though meek of mien,
In Holy Writ, with saintly sheen,
Stands thy blest name ! No sceptred queen
　　Wears diadem so bright.

9.

Therefore, where Easter altars shine,
One rose with Easter flowers entwine,
　　Her name still fresh to keep !
Children, like her—his lambs—to bear,
The Shepherd loves ; and thousands there
Follow the Lamb in pastures fair
　　Where Jesus folds His sheep.

THE WALK TO EMMAUS.

Of which salvation the prophets have inquired. . . . Searching what or what manner of time the Spirit of Christ, which was in them, did signify, when it testified beforehand the sufferings of Christ and the glory that should follow.—I St. Peter, i. 11.

Did not our heart burn within us, while He talked with us by the way and while He opened to us the Scriptures.—St. Luke, xxiv. 32.

1.

Once gazing on a craftsman's curious die
   Deep in the temper'd metal wrought,
I strove its cunning plan to spy,
   Yet seem'd to profit naught.
The quaint device was intricate and blind :
Backward the figures ran, its scheme I could not find.

2.

Smiled at my task the artist, as he came
   Bearing embossed a golden shield ;
Its rich devices flashed like flame
   And in its light, revealed,
I saw the mystery and sublime intent
That in the matrice dark me foiled with wonderment.

3.

Great God thy wondrous ways and work obscure
   Seem'd in that happy art exposed :

Dropt from mine eyes the scales impure
  That Faith's clear eyesight closed.
Of dim prophetic signs I felt the scope,
And saw, the veil withdrawn, thy glorious counsels ope.

4.

Before all worlds, Faith's shield of shining gold
  With God's device was glorified,
Where wondering angels might behold
  The Lamb of God that died ;
There stood His cross, with types to intertwine,
Tokens so rich and rare, enwreathed with His true Vine.

5.

That shield the Gospel shows in all its light ;
  But till that came—the matrice dark
God gave to be explored, by night,
  As 'twere the Holy Ark
Within the veil,—a mystery sublime,
To be devoutly kept for His appointed time.

6.

So, all that hoary seers and prophets gave,
  All that by lips inspired was sung
In Salem's royal halls, by Chebar's wave,
  Or Uzzian rocks among ;
First, in the Gospel's gold I rightly scan ;
Then trace the mould obscure to find the Son of Man.

7.

So, while I gaze, how burns within my heart,
  Though all around me owlets hoot,
To scan the emblems of the graver's art,
  Olive and vine and fruit,
Enfolding and emblazoning the cross,
Incisions deeply sunk and dark inverted boss.

8.

The backward letters of the groping Jew,
  Thus searching out I read aright ;
Mosaic symbols strange and dim to view
  Now flash with Tabor's light ;
The mystic seal by what it stamps is known,
The Gospel in the Law by prophecy foreshown.

9.

O fools and slow of heart, as Jesus said,
  Are they, of dullard wit and cold,
Who set their barren brains and lore of lead
  Against this lore of gold.
Reading Mosaic mould and prophet's page
All uncompared with Christ and His foretoken'd
  Age.

10.

For me, not so the prophets' goodly band
  Unfold the characters they traced ;
Which ev'n their ken might fail to understand,
  Till all by Faith embraced,

Searching of what and whose blest days they
    sung,
While Christ himself within inspired each rap-
    turous tongue.

11.

Great pupil of Gamaliel, oft with thee,
    As at thy saintly feet I learn,
I seem, outshining noontide, Christ to see,
    And His dear cross discern,
Where, but for thee, and thine anointed eyes,
Naught but dull forms abound and senseless
    sacrifice.

12.

Or walking to Emmaus, with the twain,
    'Neath the first Easter's Evening Star,
Me Christ draws near, nor shows his hands in
    vain,
    And in His side the scar,
Sprinkling the Book with hyssop and with gore,
That so who runs may read and live forever-
    more.

THE EARTHQUAKE.

THERE was a great earthquake.—ST. MATT. xxviii. 2.
Early in the morning.—Ps. v. 3.
I myself will awake right early.—Ps. lvii. 9.

1.

THE sun leaps up the golden skies,
  And seems to say,
Ev'n so the Son of God did rise
  On Easter-Day :
Then early from my bed let me
 Rise on the Resurrection Morn;
The dancing sunbeams let me see
 Soon as the joyous feast is born.
  Yes, early to the church away :
  'Tis Easter-Day, 'tis Easter-Day !

2.

The moon went down, and in the dark
  The garden lay,
Nor yet had lifted wing the lark
  That Easter-Day,
When holy women, as they went
 To seek the glorious slumberer,
Felt, as if earth itself were rent,
 The shock that shook the sepulchre :
  For leap'd the mountains far away,
  That Easter-Day—that Easter-Day.

3.

Tabor and Hermon skipped like rams
    In gladsome May ;
And leap'd the little hills like lambs,
    That Easter-Day.
From Libanus, like thunder heard—
  That rumbles in the distant sky,
Came sounds as if the mountains stirr'd
  To lift their hoary heads on high.
      Trembled the earth at morning's ray,
      That Easter-Day—that Easter-Day.

4.

For then, as with the lightning's stroke,
    Was roll'd away
The massy stone ; and God awoke,
    That Easter-Day !
Frightened the Roman sentries fell,
  Then fled as from the day of doom ;
They heard the rending gates of hell,
  They saw a birth from morning's womb :
      Forth shone the Christ, to live for aye,
      That Easter-Day—that Easter-Day.

5.

What ailed thee, ocean ? Saw, and fled
    Thy waves away !
And Jordan—vanished from its bed,
    That Easter-Day.
Nature's untutored worshipper
  Who deemed his god was dead, yestreen,

Far off at sea—poor mariner,
  Cried—"the Great Pan revives, I ween,"
    For so the pagan, in his way,
    Kept Easter-Day—kept Easter-Day.

6.

But not those gracious women turn'd,
  Not they! Not they!
Brighter their faith within them burned.
    That Easter-Day.
And now the flying guards they met,
  And now the garden's wall was nigh;
There stood the ghastly crosses yet;
  They saw, and uttered with a sigh—
    "But who shall roll the stone away?"
    'Twas Easter-Day, 'twas Easter-Day.

7.

Then came of faith the great reward:
    Begone dismay!
Angels they met—not yet their Lord—
    That Easter-Day.
"Here seek Him not"—the angels said—
  "The Lord is risen; search not here!
Why seek the living 'midst the dead?
  Go tell His flock the Lord is near,
    Behold the place where Jesus lay!"
    'Twas Easter-Day—'twas Easter-Day.

8.

Then, like those Marys, let us rise,
    Ere morning's ray,

Before the dayspring greets our eyes
   On Easter-Day ;
Forth to His altar, hasten we
  Where faith beholds His presence sweet,
For Christ is with His two or three,
  That worship at the mercy-seat.
      Right early let us wake to pray,
      On Easter-Day—on Easter-Day !

THE MYSTERY OF LIFE.

Dost thou show wonders among the dead?—PSALM, lxxxviii. 10.
How are the dead raised up?—I. COR. xv. 35.

1.

MASTER, we see Thy signs,
The wonders wrought by Thee, yet fail in faith;
Thy power of life we see, yet cling to death,
   Like those who dwell in mines,
   And burrow like blind moles ev'n where the daylight shines.

2.

Saviour, Thy signs we see,
In things discovered late by human thought,
But proudly claim'd, as if by mortals wrought,
   Though all vouchsafed by Thee—
   And given in Thy good time, as Time's occasion be.

3.

Why, if the human mind
Moves of itself and is its own quick spring,
Is progress slow to mark the simplest thing?
   Why, for long ages blind—
   Where God points out the way—lags mortal wit behind?

4.

Thou givest power to men
To stretch their wiry fibres 'neath the sea,
And bid the lightings go, in mimicry
    Of power divine. Why then
      Doubt we Thy power to work beyond our feeble ken?

5.

Thus, in Thy days below,
Thy word ran swiftly, and was felt afar
Like arrowy rays of sun or faintest star,
    Soothing a sufferer's woe:
      No need of clumsy wires to bid Thy lightings go!

6.

A father told his grief,
And in a moment, on his bed of pain,
The lov'd one, far away, felt life again;
    Of sons of men the Chief
      Gave but His word to heal and came the swift relief.

7.

We note the comet's blaze:
Nay—Thy sweet law makes music 'mid the spheres;
Yet in the ordered course of days and years
    Men fail to see Thy ways—
      Marvels of boundless power that angels might amaze.

8.

Wonders among the dead
Thou showest when the flowery spring returns
And clothes the fields and woods with flowers
and ferns;
Or where mankind is fed
By the mere corn of wheat that multiplies
their bread.

9.

Or where the mummy's hand
Gives up perchance the grains that Joseph stored,
And lo! though ages held the secret hoard,
It lives at thy command,
And harvests of that seed are gathered from
the land.

10.

Shall God revive that corn
And not the coffin'd flesh that held, so long,
A buried thing in Death's enthrallment strong?
Shame on the fool's poor scorn,
We see in signs like these the breaking of the
morn.

EUDORA.

A gracious woman retaineth honour.—PROVERBS, xi. 16.

1.

Her smile was many smiles in one;
  As o'er the dimpled tide,
A wavy laughter seems to run,
  Where gentle waters glide.

2.

It came as comes the morning star
  Day after day so bright,
To set the pearly doors ajar,
  And usher in the light.

3.

Sweet sister! from my sight removed—
  Upon the shining shore,
So pure, so glad, so stainless proved,
  Lives then that smile no more?

4.

When angels bore her radiant sprite
  To Paradise, meseems
Her smile met theirs in calm delight,
  Commingling kindred beams.

5.

She slept and seemed to smile in sleep;
   'Twas on the Lady-Day
She went her Easter-tide to keep,
   Where Easter reigns for aye.

6.

That smile upon her features played
   When, raimented in white,
Her form in soft repose was laid,
   And seemed a saint in light.

7.

Oh! can it be, if e'er shall meet
   Again thy soul with mine,
A smile so heavenly and so sweet
   Shall be no longer thine?

8.

Transformed, but yet the same to view,
   Was Abr'am seen afar:
So Moses and Elias flew
   Anear the Morning Star;

9.

And saints that with the Saviour rose
   In their immortal sheen
Were yet the same that slept—like those
   By John in Patmos seen.

10.

All tears from off all faces—He
  The Lamb Himself shall dry,
But that sweet smile He gave to thee
  Methinks shall never die.

11.

On some, made meet for worlds more fair,
  While here they linger yet,
Not all of earth are graces rare
  That like a seal are set.

12.

And we shall know thee, still the same,
  By that transporting charm,
If but, like thine, our faith may claim
  The Everlasting Arm.

THE INNOCENTS.

Refrain thy voice from weeping and thine eyes from tears, for . thy children shall come again to their own border.—Jeremiah, xxxi. 17.

1.

Reading the stones that marked a field of death,
    I heard a sigh, as 'mid the mounds I trod :
It seem'd to say—as 'twere with sobbing breath—
    My heart is buried here, O Christ, my God !

2.

A mother by a new-made bed that knelt,
    I saw—and turned my steps with rev'rent fear ;
Yet lingering in the church-yard walks, I felt,
    Dear Lord ! how many hearts are hoarded here.

3.

How many buds and blossoms of the spring,
    By frosts too early nipp'd, lie thickly strown ;
Or like the swallows oft, on eager wing,
    That come untimely and too soon are flown.

4.

Yet 'neath these heaps of buried hopes that tell
    Are sown not less the seeds of life's return :
God's ore is treasured in each narrow cell,
    Where gold refines and only dross can burn.

5.

Oh! weep not, mother, o'er that bed of love
   Where innocence awaits the trumpet's sound,
While many a mother mourns her dead above
   And weeps no more for children under ground.

6.

But come this way when holy hymns are sung,
   And sounds the air with Paschal-anthems rife,
To charge with notes of joy thy plaintive tongue,
   And sing the Resurrection and the Life.

7.

For sweetly sleeps the chrisom-child at rest,
   And fain with such the Christian heart would lie!
If so God wills—of all His gifts 'tis best,
   Fresh from the font, in Christ new-born, to die.

THE UNBAPTIZED.

Is it well with the child? 2 KINGS, iv. 26.

1.

A LADY wept, with tears undried—
  For her bright boy who came
Only to close his eyes, and died
  Unchristen'd, with no name—
Lest he should wear no coronal divine
Among those innocents like stars of morn that shine.

2.

Is then the guiltless babe shut out
  From that palm-bearing band?
Resolve, O man of God, my doubt!
  Fain would I understand,
Where is my darling's soul, or where his lot?
Hath He no place for such, who said, "Forbid them not"?

3.

O mother, faithless are thy fears,
  Tho' sore thy faith be tried;
Triumphant hope may smile thro' tears
  And trust in Him who died;
From thine embrace of love a lamb is torn,
But on thy Shepherd's breast doubt not that lamb is borne.

4.

Thy child is His far more than thine;
   He claims it for His fold;
And grace—unfetter'd by its sign—
   Is giv'n to young and old.
'Tis no presumptuous thought, of human wit,
But lo! such light shines clear in lines of Holy
     Writ.

5.

As on its stem, all undefiled,
   The lily's bud is seen,
Hath He not said the Christian's child
   Is holy, not unclean?
For, hallow'd by the mother's faith and prayer,
With her the babe unborn is fed on angels' fare.

6.

If holy be the planted root,
   Planted in God's own ground,
Holy the flower and blest the fruit
   Upon its branches found.
Nor one poor blighted bud shall fall to earth
Too soon for Him to save who gives the second
     birth.

7.

Nor deem from Paynim fields afar
   He gleans no holy seed:
Nations that ne'er beheld His star,
   His rod and staff may lead.
Where Hagar faints—how near the angel wing
That for her dying boy reveals the hidden spring.

8.

Unnumber'd are the babes on whom
  No christ'ning dews were shed,
Who yet were His, within the womb,
  And with His flock are fed,
Who guides His sheep the living streams among,
And gently leadeth those who yet enfold their
    young.

9.

Such be thy trust, such hope be thine—
  All else is mystery.
The nameless babe let faith resign
  To Mercy's mild decree,
Full sure not woman's love itself can teach
Aught of true love to Him whose love surpasseth
    speech.

10.

Where God is silent—more to seek
  Or prompt the Holy One,
Is faithless thought. This only speak:
  Father, Thy will be done.
To save all souls that sin, the Saviour died:
For souls that never sinned, trust then the Crucified.

EUTHANASIA.

She answered, It is well.—2 Kings, iv. 26.

1.

Thee, 'mid the flowers of paradise, as fair and undefiled;
Thee, happy daughter of thy God—how dare I call thee child?
Yet let me name thee with the blest, and, though thy date was brief,
Think only of thy new estate, with joy and not with grief.

2.

So soon to leave far far below our vale of tears and pain;
Through earth so soon and bright to pass, a sunbeam without stain;
To come, and in thy Saviour's arms baptismal life to win—
Then take thy flight, a sinless one, from such a world of sin:

3.

Sure this is blessedness! How blest a ransom'd one to be,
So short thy little moment here, so long eternity!
'Tis thine, on wings unstained as theirs, to soar with cherubim,
Yet, with a love no angel knows, Redemption's song to hymn!

4.

Thou blue-eyed darling of my soul—from such a life divine,
Sweet Dora, could I call thee down to share a life like mine?
Or could we pray for thy return to selfish eyes and arms,
Thine the hard lot of earth to bear—and ours thy captive charms?

5.

Nay, let me rather share with thee thy life of joy and love!
Part of my flesh is in thy grave—part of my soul above;
And oft in dreams I seem to rest, since thou art gone before,
Where the Good Shepherd folds the lambs that once in arms He bore.

6.

Yet can it be, for oft such thoughts of bitterness upspring,
That such as I, with such as thou, the Lamb's new song may sing?
That I with thee, in Paradise, may walk in robes that shine,
And share th' eternal marriage-feast with virgin souls like thine?

7.

So turns my spirit, Lord, to Thee, as with his aching sight,
Who from thy crimsoned cross received a welcome into light;
And for a childlike heart, once more, my inmost nature cries,
To Thee—alone who wipest tears forever from our eyes.

8.

Oh! let not hopes that heavenward soar be thrust adown to hell;
These hopes of immortality, this thirst with Thee to dwell;
But, out of longings after life, let Thy sweet Spirit give
Strength to assert our destiny and by Thy life to live!

9.

Ev'n as young wings are stretch'd for flight while plumeless in the nest;
As dreaming babes with rosy lips invite the balmy breast;
As flowers uplift the fragrant cup ere evening's dews are given,
So faith, with all its pure desires, foretells its home in heaven.

10.

Dear Lamb of God, though far below the dear
    one of my heart,
Be mine at least the sight of those who see Thee
    as Thou art,
And grant me but the meanest place among the
    glorified ;
For whom have I in heaven but Thee, or what
    on earth beside ?

A THOUGHT FROM THE FATHERS.

My burden is light.—S. MATT. xi. 30.

1.

SEE how yon little lark is borne
   With music up to heaven,
To bask in sunlight ere the morn
   To vales beneath is given.

2.

That bird salvation's sign hath made
   By stretching forth his wings;
The cross upon his back is laid,
   And lo! he soars and sings.

3.

Take off the fardel that he bears,
   He falleth in his flight;
The cross *is* in the wings he wears;
   He proves the burden light.

4.

So Christ hath laid His cross on me;
   It wings me to the sky,
And day by day, though sore it be,
   By that dear cross live I.

5.

It beareth those by whom 'tis borne ;
   And by its weight we rise.
Who casts it down, he sinks forlorn ;
   Who takes it up, he flies.

6.

Easy the yoke, and light the load,
   Indeed, my spirit sings ;
To him that pants for God's abode,
   His cross shall prove his wings.

AMARANTH.

We have forsaken all.... what shall we have therefore?
—S. Matt. xix. 27.

1.

Be still, my fluttering heart, nor dim
    The flame of faith divine;
But say—All things are mine in Him
    If only Christ be mine.

2.

Not here are amaranthine bowers;
    But, loving and forgiven,
Thine yet shall be, for earthly flowers,
    Their antitypes in heaven.

3.

Not all to mock our waking sight
    Fair forms in sleep we view;
But oft our visions of the night
    Are figures of the true.

4.

Then look beyond, with sweet content,
    When, o'er the April sky,
Is seen that arch of glory bent
    Which glitters but to die.

5.

Not all unseen, not all unknown,
    Are things within the veil;
There is a rainbow round the throne,
    Whose hues nor fade nor fail.

6.

There's not a bliss we sigh for here
    That is not kept above,
Pure as the heavenly atmosphere,
    For hearts that Jesus love.

7.

There's not a toy that is cast down
    By souls the cross that bear,
That helps not to the glittering crown
    Reserved in glory there.

8.

And if the restless heart we tame
    Its idols to forego,
Treasures of love, in Christ's dear name,
    The Father will bestow.

9.

For, sure as in the soul are powers
    Which here we must restrain,
There's something that shall yet be ours
    To prove them not in vain.

THE ASCENSION.

Oh that I had wings like a dove! for then would I fly away, and be at rest.—Ps. lv. 6.

1.

Like shapes the mirror's depth within,
   That, in their fashions, come and go,
A world that is not, nor hath been,
   Of phantoms passing to and fro;

2.

Ev'n thus unreal and as vain,
   The scene that mocks the human eye,
Where pomp, with flattery in its train,
   Struts forth, or flaunts disdainful by.

3.

I saw an empire's rise and fall;
   Its monstrous birth, its hasty end;
One rose and reigned and ruined all,
   Himself and all that call'd him friend.

4.

Not such His realm who bore the reed
   Of mock'ry in His mighty hand;
Who stooped to suffer and to bleed,
   But rose to reign o'er every land;

5.

Who bowed to taste the wayside rill,
   That mock'd His thirst ; then raised His head
With living streams the world to fill,
   And light and life o'er all to shed ;

6.

Who rose the gates of bliss to ope,
   And bids us rise His throne to share :
Like Him to die and rest in hope,
   Like Him to reign in glory there.

7.

Oh for the wings, consoling Dove,
   Thou lendest to the spirit pure,
To flee away and soar above,
   To worlds of glory that endure !

THE UNSPEAKABLE GIFT.

SHALL He not, also, with Him, freely give us all things?
—ROM. viii. 32.

1.

Oh Thou whose blood my soul to heal
As Gilead's balm, at times I feel,
Saviour divine, I find Thee more
Than I had thought, or dreamed, before;
Content, if but such bliss may be,
To breathe, and move, and live in Thee.

2.

My soul is dark, be Thou my day,
My light within and on my way;
Athirst and faint, I find Thee still
Like Silo's fount, or Kedron's rill;
Or if by hunger's pang subdued,
Bread of the soul, Thou art my food.

3.

When howls the storm, my safe retreat;
My shelter from the burning heat,
My anchor when the billows rise,
My soaring wing to brighter skies;
All this and more, Thee, Lord, I call,
My Light, my Life, my all in all.

THE UNSPEAKABLE GIFT.

4.

And oft, dear Lord, in sorest need,
On barren husks enforced to feed,
Be mine the pardon'd wand'rer's lot,
And his, beside, who wandered not:
A home in Thine embrace divine,
Ever with Thee and all things mine.

THE TWO PENTECOSTS.

I will make all my goodness pass before thee.—Exod. xxxiii. 19.

1.

O Sinai ! dark and thunder-scarr'd,
How oft, as in a dismal dream,
　Thy clouded heights so hard,
Before my sight uplifted seem,
With cavern'd sides and clefts extreme ;
　Gigantic quarry of the Law,
Womb of those stony slabs austere
　Whereon I read with awe
Letters of fire and flame that fill my soul with fear.

2.

　Yet even here, on Law's dread throne,
Whence came the thunder and the ban,
　Ev'n here was mercy shewn ;
Mercy and love to sinful man,
When Moses long'd God's bliss to scan
　For comfort not revealed to sense,
And cried : Thy glory let me trace.
　Oh ! for that joy intense ;
Shew me, O Lord, I pray, the glory of Thy face.

3.

　Comes the blest answer, o'er and o'er,
In echoes from that awful Rock ;

> Hear it, and evermore
> Rejoice, poor erring, cowering flock,
> Stunn'd by the trumpet and the shock—
>   Hear Mercy's promise, even there,
> Soft as He spake on Calvary's tree
>   Of Paradise so fair :
> Goodness my glory is—that will I shew to Thee.

4.

>   He changeth not. Long years had pass'd,
> And lo ! Elijah thither came ;
>   Came to those caverns vast,
> 'Mid earthquake, winds, and lightning's flame,
> To know—if God were still the same,
>   Tho' Israel's foul idolatries
> Cried from the ground, invoking ire ;
>   Soft as the summer's breeze
> The still small voice was His : God spake not in
>   the fire.

5.

>   So on that mount of Pentecost,
> Whence came the fiery Law of Death,
>   O God, the Holy Ghost,
> Came words of Life, came Thy soft breath,
> As when a mother comforteth
>   The child her loving arms enfold.
> That still small voice was Power and Might ;
>   Backward the thunders rolled,
> And came the cloven tongues of Love and Life
>   and Light.

WHITSUNDAY.

There were seven lamps of fire burning before the throne, which are the seven Spirits of God.—Rev. iv. 5.

1.

Breath of the Lord, O Spirit blest,
Inspiring Guide, consoling Guest,
Thy perfect gifts and lights to lend,
On mortal heads and hearts descend;
Come to the sluggish sense and mind
As comes the rushing, mighty wind.

2.

Come, Promise of the Holy One;
Come, Paraclete of God the Son;
Come like the Spring's reviving gale
To furrowed soil or flagging sail;
Or come as first Thy presence came,
With fiery tongues of cloven flame.

3.

Spirit of power, come down; draw near,
Spirit of truth and holy fear;
Succour poor souls that strive with sin,
The foes without, the foe within:
And, like the morning's sun, dispel
The shades of death, the powers of hell.

WHITSUNDAY.

4.

Spirit of Christ our Paschal Lamb,
On mortal wounds come pour Thy balm;
To fainting flesh the oil supply
That heals the soul, that opes the eye;
The sinner's broken heart restore,
Forgiven much that loves the more.

5.

Dove of the Lord, with brooding wings
Creative o'er created things,
Come build anew thy peaceful nest
Where sorrows vex the human breast;
There 'mid its thorns thy note be heard—
The turtle's voice, the Spirit's Word.

6.

Fire of the Lord and Light Divine,
Thou glory of th' Eternal Trine,
Come and this gloomy world inflame,
With Jesus' love, Jehovah's name,
And, from those lamps before the throne,
Send sevenfold radiance all thine own.

7.

River of Life, make all things new;
Come, flow the thirsty fallows through;
From sweet Siloam's fount, above,
Shed showers of grace, shed dews of love;
Come, spread thy living streams abroad;
Make glad the city of our God.

HOMEWARD.

> TOILING in rowing, for the wind was contrary.—S. MARK, vi. 48.

1.

BREATH of the Lord, come, Holy Ghost!
Come speed me to the heavenly coast,
    Me, weary at the helm;
Helpless alike in storm or calm
To reach the soul's sure port I am,
    And fears like seas o'erwhelm.

2.

To breast the tide and shun the shore,
Vainly I toil with faithless oar,
    And drifts my bark so frail.
Breath of the Lord, O Spirit, come!
Come waft me to my heavenly home,
    And swell my drooping sail!

THE GIVER OF LIFE.

The Spirit of Life in Christ Jesus.—Rom. viii. 2.

1.

Come, Breath of God ; come, breath of lives
Whose kiss the life of man revives ;
Come and my sinful flesh restore
Like his who bathed seven times of yore.

2.

Come, Balm of God ; come, Gilead's balm ;
Come seek me, outcast that I am ;
Come pour Thyself into my mind,
Its wounds to heal, its rents to bind.

3.

Come, Dew of Heaven ; O Spirit, come,
To call my wandering spirit home ;
My senses touch, inspire, refine,
Restore the likeness lost, to Thine.

4.

My body, mind and spirit, Lord,
To these Thy life and love afford ;
Giver of Life alone art Thou,
Spirit of God, to whom we bow.

THE TRINITY.

HYMN OF THE EARLY CHRISTIANS AT CANDLE-LIGHT.

At eventide it shall be light.—ZECHARIAH, xiv. 7.

1.

Messiah, Thou brightness benign,
  Of the Holy One, image express;
O Jesu, Thou glory divine,
  Of the Father of Lights, whom we bless,
    While sunlight grows dim,
      Our eventide hymn
        Shall be thine.

2.

Now twinkles the starlight in heaven,
  The day dieth out in the west,
While kindle our lamps for the even,
  Our songs shall to Thee be address'd.
    Father, Spirit, and Son,
      Thy name trine and one
        Shall be blest.

3.

Son of God, ever-blest life bestower,
  Our well-spring and day-spring most bright,

Holy voices of saints Thee adore,
   And the world, both by day and by night :
   All times are Thine own :
   Thou art worthy alone,
         Light of light.

NOTES.

I.

THE EASTER FESTIVAL has, of late years, commended itself to the Christians of America and even to the people more generally. It is more and more religiously observed, and it is popularly recognized in all parts of our country. This indicates a great religious revolution ; for, in the boyhood of the writer, it seemed to be almost unknown in New England, where he passed some of his school-days ; while in New York, where his childhood and youth were chiefly spent, it was devoutly observed only by Churchfolk, and the remnant of the old settlers from Holland. The fact that it was also kept, in their way, by members of a foreign communion perpetuated a narrow prejudice against it. So that the inspiration of a popular feeling favourable to the nationalizing of the Easter Feast, if not of the solemnities preceding it, has been the work of "the little leaven" imparted to American Christianity by the Anglo-American Church.

Very early in life it occurred to the author that he might do something to teach his countrymen the great importance, to a great people, of Christian observances, harmonized with historic Christianity. In a country where all is raw and recent, the only hold upon the past which is essential to a normal development of its future, must be supplied by the grand system of the "Christian Year." Of this system history is full. The Literature and Laws of Christian Nations are entwined with it; nay, it is interwoven with Christian civilization in all its forms. Hence, to have no associations with it is to be provincialized and cut off from those sympathies with the remote and the ancient which Dr. Johnson so justly recognized as exalting a people in the scale of intelligent being.

Such convictions prompted the *Christian Ballads*. They were written in boyhood, and were not designed to open "the Inner Temple" of our Holy Religion. They celebrated the external beauties and perfections of the Holy Catholic Church, in its primitive simplicity and purity.

But it was not altogether unfairly said of the *Ballads*, that they were lacking in the spirit of practical piety. So it might be said of the tree, or the flower, that these are not the fruit. The *Ballads* were only designed to set forth "the Beautiful Gate" of the Temple, as an introduction to the holy places. They embellished the doorway, and invited the multitude within, and that was all.

This book is the supplement to that. It is designed to offer those who enter something more substantial, if indeed they hunger and thirst after righteousness. In the former work, Wisdom cried in the streets and proclaimed that she had builded her house; in this she speaks to her guests, within her doors: " Eat of my Bread, and drink of the Wine which I have mingled." Such, at least, is the plan and purpose of the two books, as compared and contrasted.

In a great measure, the *Christian Ballads* have served their purpose. The architecture, the manners and customs, the idealized completeness of the Prayer-book system which they portrayed, were things unknown in America, except in books and pictures, and in the exceptional case of pious Churchmen who had travelled in Europe. The book appealed to the imagination and was warmly received, and for fifty years has continued to be published, here and also in England, where, I am assured, it led to many transformations which have been wrought during the past generation. But what it essayed to picture to the imagination is now part of common routine and daily observation. Besides, it has been imitated, and has lost freshness. Much that it commends has been spoiled by overdoing and by petty details in which good taste perishes. Our national disposition to exaggerate and work a good idea to death, always reacts, till appetite is palled by satiety. It was comforting, however, to be told by a learned dignitary in England that churches now stand open everywhere, for private prayers, all the day and every day in the week, and that nothing has contributed to this result more effectually than the *Ballads*. So also said Mr. Parker, the eminent publisher.

May "the Paschal" be blest with a holier and more essential result, in making all who read it in love with the Holy Scriptures, and especially with the Church-lessons, as arranged for "the Christian Year." The history of its production is given in the proem, which is a tribute to two of my kinswomen, the precious companions of my early youth. They were alike beautiful in person and adorned with exceptional graces of mind and of Christian character. One fell asleep at Pau, where she rests under the shade of the Pyrenees, and the other, who soon followed her, reposes in a fair churchyard on the banks of the Schuylkill, near Philadelphia, where her not less lovely and highly cultivated mother is laid. Her father, my beloved uncle, who died in the military service of his country, in our late unhappy war, lies in his honoured grave near Chattanooga, in Tennessee.

II.

The Paschal New-Moon.

Page 6.—When the Paschal new-moon shines, then the devout Christian feels what is meant by the saying of Moses, that God set the sun and moon "for signs and for seasons." There are evidences in Scripture of something very much like the Paschal system existing from the beginning of human history, to display "the Lamb slain from the foundation of the world." Thus the first worship of which we have any record is that of Abel, who brought a lamb for sacrifice; and by the marginal reading we see that it was offered at an appointed time, apparently "at the end of the days." But what days? The end of the week? Or days of an appointed "season"? If the latter, ending in a day of worship and of offering a typical sacrifice of the lamb, the idea is complete. This solemnity was revived under Moses, in the institution of the Paschal, by the "ordinances of the moon." By the Paschal full-moon, therefore, was marked the time of the perfect sacrifice which the Son of God made upon the cross: and ever since it has marked the Christian Paschal, or the Holy Week and Easter.

The Council of Nice, A.D. 325, gave us the rules for calculating Easter, which are still observed, and which are found in our Prayer-books. The whole system of the Moveable Feasts in each year is regulated by these canons, and the Paschal full-moon is the pivot on which all turns. Modern astronomy owes its existence largely to the impulse given to the study of this science by the Nicene Council, especially at Alexandria, whose bishop was charged with the duty of making the annual calculations and sending through all the world the date of the next Easter. This he did in the Epiphany Season.

Page 7.—*The Church hath calendar'd thy time.* There has always been a great charm for me in this fact, the response of the Church to the "ordinances of the moon," by giving them a moral and sacred significance through all time. The Moveable Feasts introduce a beautiful variety into our years of life; and I have noted the pleasure children experience with a new almanac, to find out when Easter falls in the new year, and so, also, when the Whitsun-feasts will be due.

Page 7.—*The bow of Joseph.* The dying Jacob, in his incomparable ode, treats of Joseph as a type of Christ, and "his bow" is connected with the mention of "the Shepherd, the Stone of Israel."—Genesis, xlix. 24. And it is noteworthy that where Joseph's name appears in the corresponding ode of Moses, "the precious things *put forth by the moon*" are marked in Joseph's blessing. Were not these the "precious promises" of the Paschal?—Deut. xxxiii. 14.

III.

Prophecy.

Page 9.—In this poem I have done little else than paraphrase an incomparable figure of Archbishop Leighton. "In the whole course of my studies," says Coleridge, "I do not remember to have read so beautiful an allegory; so various and detailed, and yet so just and natural." Leighton's Works, Vol. III. p. 99. Ed. 1870.

Page 9.—*Sweet Spring.* See Genesis, ii. 10. "A river went out from Eden to water the garden, and from thence it was parted and became into four heads." See also how the Eternal Eden supplies that of which this was only the figure: the "river of water of life, clear as crystal, proceeding out of the throne of God and of the Lamb."—Rev. xxii. 1. So the Psalmist: "There is a river the streams whereof shall make glad the city of God."—Ps. xlvi. 4.

Page 9.—*Four mighty streams.* "The early Church," says West of Nairn, in his precious edition of Leighton, "understood this river to mean the Gospel of Christ, sent into the four corners of the world and contained in the writings of the four Evangelists." So St. Jerome very beautifully expounds it: and the four sections of the cross are often identified with this same geographical idea.

Page 10.—*The Serpent's head.* This text (Gen. iii. 15) is the well-head of Scripture, of prophecy, and narrative; it is the original Gospel.

Page 10.—*That sea above.* The sea of glass (Rev. iv. 6) is spoken of, and yet there shall be "no more sea."—Rev. xxi. 1. The bitter and boisterous sea we know here shall be no more, but peace and tranquillity shall be there unbounded and vast and clear as glass, and so far like a sea.

Page 10.—*Flooding the world.* Compare Ecclesiasticus (xxiv. 30). "I, Wisdom, also came out as a brook from a river, and as a conduit into a garden. I said, I will water my best garden, and will water abundantly my garden-bed; and lo! my brook became a river and my river became a sea."

IV.

Abel.

Page 11.—Behold the first altar and the first sacrifice of which we have any record: Abel brought, of the firstlings of his flock, a lamb for the oblation. And this he did by faith, says St. Paul; wherefore he understood that God had promised to provide the Lamb at the sacrifice for sin.

Page 12.—*The Sacrifice of Cain.* Cain despised the atonement. Such was the root-sin of his offering. He was the first Deist, who worshipped with tokens of "natural religion," and rejected revelation and the covenant of God through "the Seed of the woman." So Christ was rejected by the Jews. Compare St. Matthew, xxvii. 18, and I. John, iv. 12.

V.

Melchizedek.

Page 13.—Melchizedek is not called "a priest," but "the priest of the Most High God." This is the first appearance of the word priest in human history. All heathen priests were counterfeits, but their existence corroborates the sacred story. The Mosaic priests were *shadows* of the One only true priest, and types of His then future work. Christian priests are the *instruments* by whose hands and lips the Great High Priest does His work on earth, while He intercedes for us " within the veil," in Heaven. The argument of St. Paul (Hebrews v.—vii.) is based on Genesis, xiv. 18 and Psalms, cx. He shows that Melchizedek who appeared to Abraham was no created being; was " without father, without mother, without beginning of days or end of life " ; and this same Melchizedek, he says, "abideth a priest forever." He further explains that Melchizedek was a mere name for the apparition or similitude of " the King of Righteousness." So, " King of Salem " means " the Prince of Peace." Such is the interpretation of St. Ambrose. Other orthodox divines suppose that it was the patriarch Shem who thus appeared to Abraham ; but they agree that if so, he was but a type or shadow of the true Melchizedek. See Ambrose, *de Abraam*, i. cap. 4.

Page 9.—*Abraham saw Christ's day*. The Father of the Faithful saw him as Melchizedek, which the apostle tells us is but his name, in the similitude of an earthly king. To this event our Lord Himself seems to have referred, when He said : " Your father

Abraham rejoiced to see my day, and he saw it and was glad." So Isaac saw him in the marvellous visit of the three men, one of whom was the Angel-Jehovah. Jacob saw him, as the same angel with whom he wrestled and of whom he said, "I have seen God face to face." Moses saw him in the Burning Bush, and afterwards when he passed by on the Mount.

Joshua beheld him, at Jericho, as "the Captain of the Lord's Host," and was thus taught his own shadowy character; the true Joshua, which is the name JESUS, in its Hebrew form, being the true leader of the army of Israel, the "Lord of Hosts."

Long afterwards he was seen with the Three Children in the fiery furnace, "like unto the Son of God."

No marvel, then, that this same "Angel-Jehovah" shewed himself to the Father of the Faithful, as the great High Priest, as the King of Kings.

So beautiful the plan of God, in giving thus early to Faith a manifestation of the Messiah, God and Man.

Page 12.—*Forth comes the bread and wine.* This Eternal Priest "brings forth bread and wine": and is adored by Abraham, who pays him tithes, as an acknowledgment of his Everlasting Priesthood.

This enables St. Paul to prove that the Levitical priesthood was a mere type and shadow of a Priesthood that was before it, and should endure forever, while that of Levi's sons should pass away.

VI.

The Great High Priest.

Page 15.—*Unsired, unborn.* St. Paul expressly asserts that Melchizedek, "without father, without mother, without descent, having neither beginning of days nor end of life, . . *abideth a priest continually.*" He declares this of the same Melchizedek who met Abraham; and he tells us that the similitude "King of Salem," means only that He is "the Prince of Peace," as the name Melchizedek means only that He is the King of Righteousness. The parenthesis, "*made like* unto the Son of God," no more affects the sense than when it is said in Daniel, "One *like the Son of Man* came with clouds."

Page 16.—*God's fellow.* "The man that is My fellow, saith the Lord of Hosts" (Zech. xiii. 7).

Page 16.—*Ancient of Days.* In Daniel's vision we behold the Royal Priest more expressly portrayed, of whom Zechariah says, "He shall be a Priest upon His throne."

Page 16.—*Of Ages the Great Rock* (Isaiah, xxiv. 4). We should read the margin of our bibles and the texts there cited for comparison. This true and close rendering of the Hebrew is only in the margin of our English version.

VII.

Marah.

Page 17.—The name of Mary is found in the Old Testament in Marah, and in Miriam. The poem designs to show how highly symbolical are these names, and how truly prophetic. For Marah, see Exodus, xv. 23.

Page 17.—*The Branch* (Jeremiah, xxiii. 5; also, Zech. iii. 8, and vi. 12). The Branch is a name of Christ, and occurs in many places of Holy Scripture. Notably, as we learn in the margin of our bibles, "the Dayspring" of St. Luke, i. 78, may be rendered the Branch, or the Sunrising.

18. *Marah* and *Miriam*. These, like *Maria* and *Mary*, are forms of the same name; and we find both together in the story of the first Paschal (Exodus, xv. 20). So, too, Miriam's leprosy (Numbers, xii. 10) expresses, as Marah does, the bitter taint of our natural sinfulness, and the Branch is again brought into view, as the Healer. The Mosaic System begins with this significant introduction of the hidden Christ: "I am the Lord that healeth Thee." All its symbolism rebukes the false idea of "the Immaculate Conception" of Mary, and shows that this destroys one of the root-principles of the Gospel. It seems to have originated with Mohammed.

Page 17.—*With healing in his wings*. The Dayspring, as I have said, is also the Branch; and the healing Branch seems coupled with "the Sunrising," in the prophetic promise of Malachi, iv. 2, "Unto you that fear my name shall the Sun of Righteousness arise with healing in his wings."

Page 18.—*The Magnificat*, though very naturally connected with Christmas, is, in fact, an Easter-song, and such is the song of Miriam, with which connects the Eternal Paschal hymn (Rev. xv. 3), called "the Song of Moses and of the Lamb." We celebrate the

Conception of our Lord, in close connection with the Paschal season, on the 25th of March, and that is the date of the *Magnificat.* Christ's suffering, at this time, the Fathers say, was "like the kid seethed in his mother's milk." In this fanciful way they illustrate the cruelty of those who crucified the Lord, in the presence of His mother, and at the time of His Annunciation.

Page 18.—*Of Gilead's Tree.* The forests of Gilead abounded in spice-bearing shrubs and balsamic trees. Jeremiah, viii. 22, is therefore beautifully suggestive of the tree of Marah, and its medicinal power, as also of the Good Physician.

Page 18.—*Reigns from the Tree.* The Cross is made Messiah's throne, and I have made use of an old reading of Psalm xcvi. 10, of which some of the Primitive Fathers were very fond. Pilate's inscription on the cross was meant as derision, but it was written in three languages, as if in response to the Psalmist's words : " Tell it out among the heathen that the Lord is King." It is undoubtedly true that the Jewish Scribes altered their copies of the Scriptures in no less than eighteen places, two, at least, of which were meant to obliterate prophecies of the Crucifixion. See Pearson on the Creed, art. iv., p. 335.

Thus Tertullian (against Marcion, iii. 19) says : "*The Lord reigneth from the Tree,* means Christ, who overcame death by His suffering on the Cross, and thence reigned—as death reigned before, *from Adam to Moses.*" So also Justin Martyr, who accuses the Jews of erasing the words he quotes from the Psalms : " *The Lord hath reigned from the wood ;* but no one of your people ever reigned thus, save only He who was crucified, and who now liveth and reigneth among the nations." I condense my quotation—for he goes on to quote the whole Psalm. He seems to connect with this idea the twelfth verse, "Then shall all the trees of the wood rejoice before the Lord," as if the very trees could rejoice that the wood of the Cross was transfigured into the Tree of Life. See *Ante-Nicene Fathers* (Am. Edition, Buffalo and New York, 1885-6), Vol. I. p. 176, n. 4, also p. 235; and Vol. III. p. 337, n. 3.

VIII.

Paschal Emblems.

Page 29.—For Cain's oblation, see Note IV.

Page 29 —*On Jacob's dying eye.* The reader will please turn to the incomparable dithyrambic ode of the dying Jacob (Gen xlix., verses 8, 22, 24, etc.), for the references here introduced.

Page 29.—*The Uzzian's hand* (see Job, xix. 23-27). No ingenuity has been able to rob this superb passage of its Messianic character, as maintained in our English Version. Even the Revised Version sufficiently supports this, and the Septuagint alone is testimony that so it was understood before Christ came. See Dr. Pusey's *Daniel*, p. 504.

IX.

The Saviour.

Page 36.—"Joshua" is a marvellous name in the history of revealed truth. Thus, "Hoshea" becomes

"Jehoshua," by the prophetic act of Moses (Num. xiii. 16), and adds to the idea of Salvation that of Jehovah; *i.e.*, "Jehovah-Salvation." This becomes "Joshua" in the person of the typical "Jesus," referred to in Heb. iv. 8. Now, the angel gives this name at last to Him who was the end of types: "Thou shalt call His name JOSHUA (Jesus), for He shall *save* His people *from their sins*." The divine Saviour, "Jehoshua," combines the names "Jehovah" and "Salvation."

X.

A Hymn of Faith.

Page 53.—The intolerably prosaic character of vulgar minds is often outrivalled by the dulness of strong intellects if they are merely mechanical in their operations. This hymn celebrates the domain of Faith; not as hostile to Science, but as illuminating Science, and yet restraining Imagination. There are those who cannot smell the most fragrant flower, and many cannot distinguish colours; so, others have no ear for music. All nature with its "incense-breathing" seasons, and its profusion of radiant tints at morn and even, is lost on such minds. What can they see in the intense poetry of Scripture? The lyrics of the prophets are full of Pindaric touches and allusions which are lost on them, because we cannot make them express anything, mathematically. Instead of enjoying a rose, they bring a crucible or a retort and treat it chemically, finding nothing in it but so much carbon. In spite of such critics, we enjoy a garden, and we find it in Scripture.

XI.

Holy Week.

Page 61.—The Church, with true instinct, reads this prophecy of Isaiah (lxiii. 1) in Holy Week, and in close connection with Palm Sunday. Many imagine that it should be kept till Easter week, because it foretells the Conqueror. The answer is—That is precisely what Palm Sunday foretells; it antedates the victory, and does not admit that the triumph is less certain on Palm Sunday than on Easter Day. The prophet descries the dyed garments, before they were dyed, and this he intimates when he drops the prophetic future of history and adopts the grammatical future, in the words—" their blood *shall be sprinkled* upon my garments, and *I will stain* all my raiment." The whole passage mixes the future and the historic on a familiar principle of prophecy, which "calleth those things which be not as though they were" (Rom. xviii. 17). In these verses this view is taken of the two prophecies ; Zechariah depicts the scene as it should occur, the meek and lowly Nazarene coming to Jerusalem on the ass's foal ; Isaiah, as it should be seen by faith, "the Lamb slain from the foundation of the world," and in that view full of wounds and blood-stains, while also the Lion of the tribe of Judah, and not less the Conqueror, from the foundation of the world.

Palm Sunday, then, receives its double character from this twofold view. As the first day of Holy Week, the Sunday of the Cross, it borrows a profoundly sombre and penitential cast from the succeeding days; and yet, as the Hosanna Sunday and the Day of Palms, it is a festival in which the Victim and the soldier are already seen, by faith, as the glorified Priest and the Conqueror with dyed garments, whose triumph was sure, from the foundation of the world.

XII.

The Messiah.

Page 63.—The "Anointed One," for such is the sense of the Hebrew *Messiah* and the Greek *Christ*, is here conceived of as recognized by Mary of Bethany in her loving act, which was inspired possibly by the remarkable passage from the Canticles here prefixed as a motto. He had accepted such a tribute from the "woman which was a sinner." She now offers a like anointing on the part of "the virgins," and to show their love.

XIII.

The Betrayer.

Page 69.—The ancient church at Speyer has been recently "restored" with costly and even magnificent want of judgment. It has become a modern church to all intents, and is no unfair symbol of the Latin Church as modernized by the recent "new dogmas" which have been so fatal to her catholicity. But the quaint old mound in the south precinct has been restored in a manner which, no doubt, faithfully reproduces the mediæval effect of the original, and it is very striking when seen in a moment of loneliness and meditation. The poem is a truthful statement of the impressions it seems capable of producing on a thoughtful visitor.

XIV.

The Council.

Page 75.—*Come, then, pedestrian Muse.* There are occasions when "pedestrian" art, thus recognized by Horace, becomes legitimate in poetry. I have felt that my desire to render that famous passage in the Book of Wisdom, as literally as the form of verse will permit, furnishes a just occasion for the invocation here introduced. It is a pity that any Christian should not feel the force of such a scripture, though Apocryphal, as proving that Isaiah and other prophets had sufficiently forewarned the Jews of their great peril, in the day of Messiah's coming. See Archbishop Leighton on Ps. xxxix. 10, and the Note in West's edition, Vol. V. p. 62. Compare Plato, *Republic*, II. 5; and Cicero, *Republic*, III. 17. It is not improbable that Plato, thinking of his master, Socrates, had yet been influenced by learned Jews to moralize as he does so prophetically. Jones of Nayland (Lect. ix.) has a striking passage on Plato's "Just One" (Works, ed. 1801, Vol. IV. p. 206).

XV.

Pontius Pilate.

Page 80.—*Some say he was a Teuton.* The idea that Pilate was from Mayence was current in an old legend, and has been revived of late by the discovery of the graves of an old Hebrew legion on the Rhine; which suggests that Jews had been quartered there, while the natives were sent to Judea, a well-known expedient of the Emperors. A governor who could talk to them in their own dialect would have suggested a reason for such transfer.

In these stanzas I have tried to treat his character as the inspired writers, and as our Lord Himself, seem to teach us to do. We must "judge nothing before the time;" and it is lawful to reflect that mercy to the "chief of sinners" may be vouchsafed through the "Chief of all the Sons of Men," whose name is Jehovah-Salvation. I have ventured to treat his case as a symbol of that of all the unevangelized; of all, in short, for whom the glorious Redeemer prayed, when He said, "They know not what they do."

XVI.

Calvary.

Page 96.—The xxv. of Isaiah is a marvellous tissue embroidered with Messianic symbols. And how striking the text here versified: "He shall spread forth His hands in the midst of them, as he that swimmeth spreadeth forth his hands to swim." The following chapter is an Easter lesson, and the third verse reads (see margin): "For the Lord Jehovah is the Rock of Ages." In the writings of Tertullian, we meet with a striking exposition of Moses' outstretched arms as an emblem of the victory of the Cross. See *Against Marcion*, b. iii. cap. 18.

XVII.

The Man of Sorrows.

Page 107.—*The child who frames a cross.* In the carpenter shop of Joseph, the child Jesus is represented by Overbeck, I suppose following older masters, as sawing out a cross, in sorrowful child-play. It is a very touching embodiment of the opinion of the Fathers, that all His life long our Lord's soul was "straitened" (St. Luke, xii. 50) by a sense of the baptism He was yet to be baptized with.

Page 107.—*Those senses five*, etc. I have here suggested the crucifixion of sense, in its specialties, as well as in its general form, as part of our Lord's sufferings. The indulgence of our senses, unchastened by self-denial and fasting, strikes me as forcibly rebuked by the meditations I have here given.

XVIII.

The Three Crosses.

Page 112.—*The Thief's Repentant Cross.* "The planet Mercury," says one, "is rarely discovered; Copernicus never saw it; it shines too near the sun. And so there is an object, in itself most luminous, which attracts too little attention, for a like reason. I mean the cross of the repentant thief, so near the cross of his Redeemer that few reflect how marvellous it is in its history, how full of instruction is the example it displays of awakened conscience and spontaneous faith, and, in short, how it glorifies the Cross of Christ itself, by manifesting its power to convert, to save, to regenerate, to sanctify, and to glorify." I quote from a sermon of my own venerated father, written and preached in his earliest professional days, which is said to have been a matchless outburst of eloquence, of feeling, and of power. This exordium has been feebly reproduced in my verses.

Page 115.—*The earth its depth*, etc. The midway stake of the cross betokens the depth and height; and the *antennæ*, the breadth of its divine Mystery, the all-embracing, the all-amazing Atonement. This is a favourite view of the Fathers.

XIX.

The Hyssop.

Page 118.—That minute event in the history of the Crucifixion—mentioned by St. John only, in the words, " and put it upon hyssop "—is one which connects the Cross with some of the most significant of the Mosaic types. For hyssop was used in sprinkling, and denoted the cleansing power of the blood of Jesus. But why so? It was foreseen, this mere *accident* of the Passion; and from this the Mosaic ritual receives its exposition. We read that Solomon "spake of trees, from the cedar tree that is in Lebanon, even unto the hyssop that springeth out of the wall;" and here note that all analogy leads us to believe that the Cross was *cedar*, while the *hyssop* is what we have said, and the *wall* is seen in Gen. xlix. 22. Joseph's blessing—his vine, overrunning the Jewish wall of separation, and blessing the outside Gentile world—alike with purifying hyssop and invigorating wine. "Purge me with hyssop," says the Psalmist. The Paschal was instituted in the sprinkling of blood with hyssop (Exod. xii. 22), and so Moses established the Old Covenant, sprinkling alike the Book and the people (Heb. ix. 19). See, also, the leper's cleansing (Levit. xiv. 4).

XX.

Nicodemus.

Page 122.—St. John introduces Nicodemus, assisting Joseph at the burial, with a reference to his first coming to Jesus by night. That most interesting story gives us no clew to the impressions with which the ruler left the Divine Teacher, but soon after (St. John, vii. 50) we read of honourable conduct which made him suspected by his fellow-Pharisees. Perhaps their words (verses 47, 48) had a slant at Nicodemus, and were meant to hint at their resolution to tolerate no defection among their number. In verse 52, they treat him with a warning in form of a question, and with a scornful reference to the Galilean teacher. What, then, was the decisive moment that brought him to discipleship? It seems to me that when he learned of the Crucifixion as an accomplished fact his mind must have recurred to (St. John, iii. 14, 15) those words, "As Moses lifted up," etc. This would have brought back all the marvellous words that followed, and which were not comprehended at the time, with a power unspeakable. They produced their effect, and

Nicodemus came forward, boldly, to claim the place to which Isaiah had summoned "the rich," so many ages beforehand (Isa. liii. 9).

XXI.

The Sepulchre.

Page 126.—I have regarded the Canticles as a storehouse of poetical imagery, applicable to the facts revealed concerning the Bridegroom and the Bride. Chapter iii. (verses 5–7) supplies the conformities I have borrowed here. From chapter ii. 7, I have borrowed the closing stanza. It may be well to note here that the Canticles are an idyllic amplification of Psalm xlv., and this must be expounded by Ephes. v. 25–33. It is to be regretted that even the Revision retains the unhappy renderings (Cant. vii. 1–3) which confound articles of the Bride's dress with the parts of the body they covered—as if the *epaulettes* of an officer were translated his "shoulders." There is strong reason to favour the idea that this idyl, while it glorifies wedded love, and proves its innocence and its mystic reference to Christ and His Church, celebrates, also, the conversion of Solomon to a life of conjugal purity and of absolute devotion to her who can say, "I am my Beloved's, and my Beloved is mine" (Cant. vi. 3).

XXII.

Easter.

Page 129.—The amazing unity of Scripture furnishes the believer a strong ground for confidence, which blind unbelief can never take away. Abel's Lamb reappears in the Apocalypse, and so does Judah's Lion; and everywhere this imagery is kept up throughout the Scriptures. This Easter-song is based upon real references and analogies. And here let the rule of heraldry be kept in view: when the Lion is emblazoned, we see only his noble and royal qualities. The cat-like treachery of the animal is reserved to describe the enemy, who "goeth about seeking whom he may devour." Now let us observe these texts:

1. It is evident that our Lord sprang out of Judah. Heb. viii. 3.
2. Judah is a lion's whelp . . he stooped down, he couched as a lion, and as an old lion; who shall rouse him up? Gen. xlix. 9.
3. The Lion of the tribe of Judah, the Root of David, hath prevailed. Rev. v. 5.

Other texts referred to, or quoted, are as follows:

1. He hath broken the gates of brass, and cut the bars of iron in sunder. Ps. cvii. 16.
2. Free among the dead. Ps. lxxxviii. 5, 7.
3. Led captivity captive. Ephes. iv. 8.
4. The lion did tear in pieces enough for his whelps. Nahum, ii. 12.
5. Christ being raised from the dead dieth no more. Rom. vi. 9.
6. A garden inclosed . . . a spring shut up, a fountain sealed. Cant. iv. 12.
7. The sting of death is sin. I. Cor. xv. 56.
8. I am tormented in this flame. Luke, xvi. 24.
9. One of the elders saith unto me, Weep not. Rev. v. 5.
10. Worthy is the Lamb that was slain. Rev. v. 12.

XXIII.

The Bird Song.

Page 135.—Describing the hills of Naphtali, says a modern traveller: "The perfume of a thousand flowers filled the air, poppies, anemones, marigold, convolvulus . . . a glowing mosaic of rainbow hues. We turned into a wild glen, where the voice of the turtle floated from tree to tree, and the cooing of countless wood-pigeons ran like a stream of soft melody along the jagged cliffs above us."—Porter's *Giant Cities*, p. 267.

XXIV.

Easter Eggs.

Page 139.—A French writer has remarked: "Toute l'antiquité s'est accordée à reconnoitre dans les oiseaux quelque chose de divin. . . Aristophane, dans sa comédie *Des Oiseaux*, fait allusion à cette tradition."

The mockery of the King of Assyria has supplied me with a text to which I have tried to give an orthodox use, taking forth honey out of a dead carcass. There is much to be said of birds; and I wonder so little has been written of these wonderful creatures, their eggs, their habits of migration, their amazing beauty, their songs, and the miracle of their triumph over gravitation, their inexplicable hold upon thin air, their power of wing, their strange life in mid-ocean, their mysterious loves and nest-buildings, their exquisite delicacy and decency of sexual formation, and the lavish hand with which God has adorned them and displayed His power in them, making them such tokens of His skill, from the humming-bird to the eagle.

XXV.

The Royal Yarn.

Page 145.—A popular travel-writer speaks frequently of the scarlet robes which are worn in Syria even in our times, as a token of rank. "The Village Sheikh," he says, "was there to welcome us, conspicuous in his scarlet robe, which, to this day, is the badge of royalty, or power, among the inhabitants of Palestine."—Porter's *Giant Cities*, p. 173.

Page 145.—*Zarah's wrist.*—Gen. xxxviii. 28. The illuminating faith of the early Christians is beautifully seen in the views of Irenæus touching this sign. He regards it as Christ's token on the seed of Judah, withdrawing its faith from Him, but still claimed by Him, for a future birth in the Gospel "This scarlet token upon Him is the passion of the Just One, prefigured by Abel, and by the prophet delineated, but in the last days perfected by the Son of God."—Irenæus's *Against Heresies*, iv. 2.

Page 145.—*Rahab's window.*—St. Clement says "The spies gave her a sign to this purpose, that she should display from her dwelling a scarlet thread thus making it plain that redemption should flow through the blood of the Lord, to all that believe and hope in God." Others of the Fathers give similar expositions (Joshua, ii. 18).

Page 146.—*Scarlet wool.*—Heb. iv. 19. "He took the blood of calves and of goats, with water and scarlet wool and hyssop, and sprinkled both the Book and all the people, saying, This is the blood of the Covenant."

Page 146.—*Scarlet robe.*—St. Matthew, xxvii. 28. The scarlet robe was embroidered with purple of reddish tinge, and the robe was described accordingly as purple or scarlet.

Page 146.—*The Bride.*—Cant. iv. "Thy lips are a thread of scarlet, and thy speech is comely."

The Church speaks with comely words, when her lips are baptized with the blood of the Lamb. The same Greek word which is rendered scarlet is sometimes rendered crimson, as in Isa. i. 18.

Page 146.—*The living Bird.*—Levit. xiv. 6. The rabbins tell us that the bird was bound to the cedar by the scarlet yarn.

XXVI.

Easter in Patmos.

Page 151.—*The Day the Lord had made.*—The Lord's Day pre-eminently (Ps. cxviii. 24) is the Annual Paschal, but every Lord's Day is a lesser Easter. Without attempting to settle the critical question whether it was Easter-Day when St. John saw, once more, the risen Lord, I adopt a Paschal interpretation of the whole Book, as a key to its divine imagery and intent. And such is the argument of this poem, which I humbly trust is auxiliary to its truth.

XXVII.

𝕮𝖍𝖊 𝕬𝖓𝖌𝖊𝖑𝖘 𝖔𝖓 𝖙𝖍𝖊 𝕬𝖗𝖐.

Page 154.—The Ark of the Covenant is one of the most striking testimonies to the evangelical nature of the Hebrew mysteries. It was enshrined within the veil; no eye beheld it there, save only the high priest's once a year, and even he could do this not without the most solemn purifyings and acts of atonement for himself and for the people. When carried through the wilderness, its terrible sanctity was guarded in the most remarkable manner, and awful punishments fell on those who profaned it, by curiosity or even by a too familiar care for it. May I venture here to warn against the blasphemous profaneness of making counterfeits of the Ark, and using this symbol of the Divine Presence in the rites of modern societies, as is said to be done? Compare I. Sam. vi. 19, 20, and II. Sam. vi. 6, 7. The cherubim, whose figures were wrought into the pure gold of the cover, and not screwed on to it, seem to intimate the unity of angelic and human beings in the Divine system and they were so placed as to look down upon the "mercy-seat,"—the burnished lid, resplendent with supernatural light, which closed upon the Ark, covering over the tables of the Law within. Thus was suggested the Law, with its direful threats of justice, hidden by the mercy of God, in the Atonement of Christ: a system so marvellous and comprehensive that "the angels desire to look into it" (I. Peter. i. 12). So St. James says : " Mercy rejoiceth against judgment ; " an apparent reference to the glorified mercy-seat, over against the stone tables of Law, which it hid from sight. The text which I have made a motto to this poem uplifts the same thought to the heavens. All heaven learns new lessons of the Divine Love from the salvation of sinners, and from the experiences of the Church Militant here on earth. This lends unutterable grandeur to the expressions of St. Paul, "Seen of Angels" (I. Tim. iii. 16), as applied to "God, manifest in the flesh."

XXVIII.

The Earthquake.

Page 165.—*Great Pan revives.*—The reader will recall a mysterious story of Plutarch, concerning what happened one day, in the time of Tiberius, to a party sailing on the Ionian gulf, near the Echinades. Voices in the air cried out, *Great Pan is dead;* and Christians have attributed the phenomenon to "some powers of the air," in their consternation, when the earth trembled at the death of Christ. Tiberius was alarmed when told of the incident; and this is a noteworthy fact as the one response of history to the natural inquiry, Did the Cæsar receive any intimation of the amazing event which makes his ignoble reign so memorable in human annals? May not the official report of Pilate have afforded him the real ground of his alarm when he heard this story, allowing certain "Acts of Pilate" to have been a real base for the fabrication that bears the name? See Dacier's *Plutarque*, Vol. VIII., p. 285. I have imagined a corresponding impression produced upon

Thamus (the pilot of the story) by the concussion of the air on "Easter Morning."

XXIX.

The Unbaptized.

Page 176.—*Hath He not said the Christian's child*, etc. "Else were your children unclean, but now are they holy" (I. Cor. vii. 14). "If the root be holy, so are the branches" (Rom. xi. 16). This poem is designed for the comfort of over-scrupulous consciences, and over-anxious inquirers about the heathen; of whom I have found examples in pastoral experience, among some of the best of men and women.

XXX.

A Thought for the Fathers.

Page 182.—St. Augustine is not the earliest of the Fathers to enlarge upon the text I have chosen for a motto, nor do I recollect that he anywhere follows an earlier authority in the pretty conceit of the figure of the cross made by the outstretched wings of the bird. But he thus expresses himself as to the burden: "Christ's burden hath wings, another's hath weight. If thou pluck off the wings of a bird, thou removest a sort of weight; but the more of that burden thou removest, the more to earth the bird must cleave. She flieth not, because thou hast unburdened her; give her back the weight—she flieth." See *Commentary on the Psalms*. Ps. lix. 7, African Psalter (lx. 6, Anglican). S. Aug. Opp. Tom. IV., p. 719. Paris: Migne, 1865.

St. Bernard copies the great African doctor as follows: "Leve Salvatoris onus, quo crescit amplius, eo portabilius est. Nonne et aviculas levat, non onerat pennarum sive plumarum numerositas ipsa? Tolle eas, et reliquum corpus pondere suo fertur ad ima. Sic disciplinam Christi, sic suave jugum, sic onus leve, quo deponimus, eo deprimimur ipsi: quia portat potius quam portatur." S. BERNARD. Epist. ccclxxxv. Opp. Vol. I., p. 691. Ed. Paris, 1839.

XXXI.

Amaranth.

Page 184.—*Not here are amaranthine bowers.* The flowers of June made me pensive even as a child: to see them fade so soon tortured me. I remember the thrill with which I heard my father quote those lines of Cowper's "Task":

> "The only amaranthine flower on earth
> Is virtue; the only lasting treasure—Truth."

He explained to me this word "amaranthine," and gave its etymology. The impression has never faded from my mind and heart.

Page 185.—*There is a rainbow round the throne.* Just so the evanescent splendour of the rainbow was painful, till I learned to dwell on the truth expressed in this stanza. I longed for something imperishable. I find it in the vision of Patmos: "There was a rainbow round about the throne, in sight like unto an emerald;" the mixed light of amethyst and topaz predominating. It was a spring-like rainbow, in which the fiery heats of July were not reflected; so, it seemed to me, we ought to understand it. So too the dreams of Fra Angelico and the *nimbus* of his holy ones seem to be justified in this text: "I saw another mighty angel come down from heaven, clothed with a cloud, and *a rainbow was upon his head.*" Thus Revelation struggles with human language when it speaks of the ineffable glories of the Blessed.

Page 185.—*For sure as in the soul are powers*, etc. The ninth stanza in the preceding poem aims, like this, to express a refreshing idea, which is beautifully rendered by Ancillon as follows: "Il y a dans les affections du cœur quelque chose de pur et de désintéressé, qui annonce l'excellence et la dignité de l'âme humaine."

XXXII.

The Ascension.

Page 186.—*Who bowed to taste the wayside rill.* Psalm cx. 7. After Pompey's defeat, says Plutarch, "étant arrivé à Tempe, brûlant de soif, *il se jeta à terre sur le visage, but dans la rivière*, et s'étant relevé il traversa la vallée," etc. This illustrates the idea of the Psalmist, in a manner; but Messiah bowed to taste the dark river, only to "lift up His head" and live and reign forever. See Dacier's *Plutarque*, Vol. V. p. 478.

XXXIII.

The Two Pentecosts.

Page 191.—*Goodness my glory is.* "And he said: I beseech Thee shew me thy glory. And He said, I will make all my goodness pass before Thee." Exod. xxxiii. 18, 19. The immense significance of this Scripture, where it stands, in connection with Sinai and the second inscription of the Decalogue upon tables of stone, is what the poem designs to illustrate. Compare Deut. xxxiv. 1-5. Was it not at this time that "all His goodness" was made to pass before Moses, prophetically?

Page 191.—*The still small voice,* etc. I. Kings, xix. 12. In the extremity of Israel's degeneracy Elijah goes back to Horeb, as if to ask whether "the fiery Law" would never be avenged. How significant the answer God vouchsafed: a premonition of the second and more glorious Pentecost, the mission of the Comforter.

XXXIV.

Whitsunday.

Page 192.—In connection with Isaiah, xi. 2, 3, it is instructive to observe (Rev. i. 4, iii. 1, iv. 5, and v. 6): the prominence given to the sevenfold gifts of the Spirit, in the great Prophecy of the New Covenant. This Pentecostal Hymn aims in some degree to celebrate the practical blessings of these gifts.

XXXV.

The Trinity.

Page 192.—Let me give the translation of this most ancient hymn of the Church as arranged, from Bishop Andrewes, in a modern Oxford edition :

> "O Joyful Light
> Of the Holy Glory of the Father,
> Immortal, Heavenly, Holy, Blessed,
> Jesus Christ :
> Beholding the Evening light,
> We glorify
> The Father and the Son.
> And the Holy Spirit of God.
> Worthy art Thou, in all seasons,
> With sacred voices to be hymoèd,
> Son of God,
> Giver of Hope ;
> Wherefore the world glorifieth Thee,
> O Joyful Light,
> Of the Holy Glory,
> Amen."

I have rearranged the stichometry, and ventured to repeat the first lines as a refrain at the close. I have always thought it must have been sung with such a refrain, unless, indeed, it concluded with one of St. Paul's doxologies ; which I am persuaded he often borrows from the Church's hymns. See *Ante-Nicene Fathers*, American edition, Vol II. p. 79, note 2, and p. 298.

This they sang even in the dark Catacombs. where, though they noted the accustomed hour of the day's decline, they could behold no other light than Christ's shining in their souls. Who has not seen the Christian lamps taken from their tombs, marked by the *acrostical* ΙΧΘΥΣ, and the ΧΡ, or the apocalyptic Alpha and Omega? When Padre Marchi showed me such relics in the Jesuit College at Rome—"Observe," said I to the venerable man, "how these early Christians worshipped JESUS and the Trinity, not Mary and 'the Star of the Sea'; and how closely they stuck to Holy Scripture." The Jesuit looked unutterable things; but he answered nothing to the purpose.

When I have taken one of these Christian relics in my hand, I have seemed to see some Christian vestal about to be thrown to the lions on the morrow, but trimming her lamp to go forth and meet the Bridegroom, as she chanted her sweet even-song of faith and hope—"O Joyful Light!" With this idea, please read it over. Innumerable Christians have sung it on the eve of martyrdom. It moves me to tears as I recite it with this thought. Bishop Andrewes' copy of the original Greek was found in his private prayer-book bedewed with his weeping. Take then this hymn of the martyr Christians at the close of day, as evidence of their faith and piety.

www.ingramcontent.com/pod-product-compliance
Lightning Source LLC
Chambersburg PA
CBHW021806230426
43669CB00008B/651